# The
# Conservation
# Movement
# in Norfolk

'Rare and beautiful Norfolk' as seen
by the Norwich School of painters:
James Stark (1794-1859),
Whitlingham from Old Thorpe
Grove, *oil on canvas.*

# The Conservation Movement in Norfolk

## A HISTORY

SUSANNA WADE MARTINS

THE BOYDELL PRESS

First published 2015
The Boydell Press, Woodbridge

ISBN  978 1 78327 007 1


The Boydell Press is an imprint of Boydell & Brewer Ltd
PO Box 9, Woodbridge, Suffolk IP12 3DF, UK
and of Boydell & Brewer Inc.
668 Mount Hope Ave, Rochester, NY 14620-2731, USA
website: www.boydellandbrewer.com



A catalogue record for this book is available
from the British Library

The publisher has no responsibility for the continued existence or accuracy of URLs
for external or third-party internet websites referred to in this book, and does not
guarantee that any content on such websites is, or will remain, accurate or
appropriate.


This publication is printed on acid-free paper

Book design: Simon Loxley

# Contents

## Illustrations

FRONTISPIECE: James Stark (1794-1859) *Whitlingham from Old Thorpe Grove* (by permission of Norfolk Museums Service, Norwich Castle Museum and Art Gallery).

## MAPS

The author and publishers are grateful to all the institutions and individuals listed for permission to reproduce the materials in which they hold copyright. Every effort has been made to trace the copyright holders; apologies are offered for any omission, and the publishers will be pleased to add any necessary acknowledgement in subsequent editions.

## Acknowledgements

The writing of this wide-ranging volume has been greatly assisted by the generosity of many people, some of whom are mentioned below. The Norfolk Wildlife Trust allowed me to search through their archives and provided me with a comfortable room in which to work and cups of coffee to keep me going. As always, the staff at the Norfolk Record Office were helpful and spent time finding documents which were not always easy to locate. Many individuals also gave of their time to help me. Alison Yardy of the Historic Environment Service looked out material, helped check references and made digital copies of illustrations. Robert Driscoll was particularly helpful in providing material and information about the Norfolk Broads. Richard Brook of the Forestry Commission sought out photographs and explained the role of the Forestry Commission in Breckland, and Tim O'Riordan and Peter Grimble provided information on recent environmental history. Merlin Waterson and John Sheail read early drafts of this book and provided much helpful advice. The maps were kindly drawn by Trevor Ashwin. I am also grateful to the anonymous readers for their hard work. As always, my husband Peter, whose idea this book was, has supported this project along the way. Those who have generously allowed copyright material to be reproduced as plates are acknowledged in the list of plates.

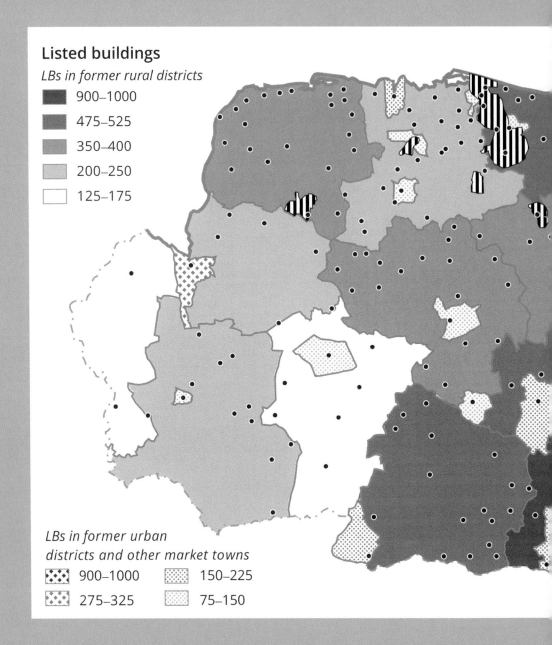

## Listed buildings

### LBs in former rural districts

- 900–1000
- 475–525
- 350–400
- 200–250
- 125–175

### LBs in former urban districts and other market towns

- 900–1000
- 275–325
- 150–225
- 75–150

## Conservation areas

IIII    Rural conservation areas

•    Village conservation areas

⓵⓼    No. of CAs in a town

0      10      20 km

*Map 1*

Map showing the statutory protection of the historic environment by the distribution of listed buildings designated by national government and conservation areas designated by local authorities.

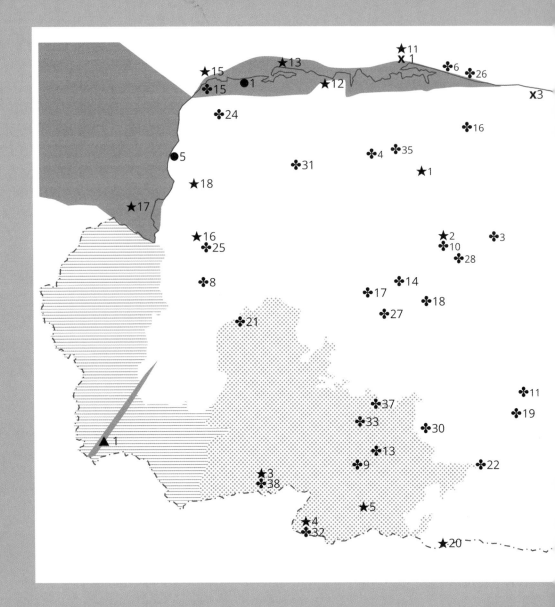

## Map 2   *Protection of the natural environment*

Map showing protection of the natural environment by both
government protection and voluntary trusts, and the main landscape
zones of Broadland, Breckland and the Fens.

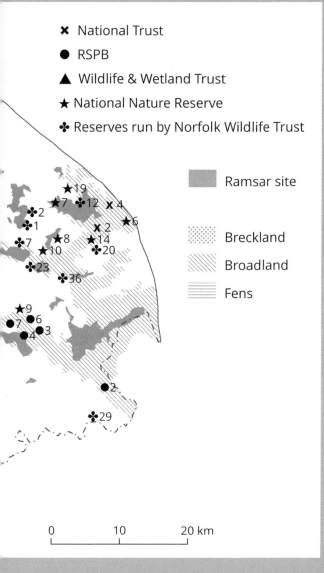

Key:

✖ National Trust
● RSPB
▲ Wildlife & Wetland Trust
★ National Nature Reserve
♣ Reserves run by Norfolk Wildlife Trust

Ramsar site

Breckland

Broadland

Fens

0    10    20 km

NATIONAL TRUST    1 – Blakeney Point;
2 – Heigham Holmes, Martham;
3 – West Runton and Beeston Regis
Heath; 4 – Horsey Estate

RSPB    1 – Titchwell; 2 – Berney Marshes;
3 – Buckenham Marshes; 4 – Rockland
Marshes; 5 – Snettisham;
6 – Strumpshaw Fen; 7 – Surlingham
(Broad)

WILDLIFE AND WETLAND TRUST
1 – Welney Washes

NATIONAL NATURE RESERVE
1 – Swanton Novers; 2 – Foxley Wood;
3 – Weeting Heath; 4 – Thetford Heath;
5 – Brettenham Heath; 6 – Winterton
Dunes; 7 – Ant Broads and Marshes;
8 – How Hill, Ludham; 9 – Mid Yare NR;
10 – Bure Marshes NR; 11 – Blakeney
Point; 12 – Holkham; 13 – Scolt Head
Island; 14 – Martham Broad; 15 – Holme
Dunes; 16 – Roydon Common;
17 – The Wash; 18 – Dersingham Bog;
19 – Calthorpe Broad; 20 – Redgrave and
Lopham Fen

NORFOLK WILDLIFE TRUST
1 – Alderfen Broad; 2 – Barton Broad;
3 – Booton Common; 4 – Brett's Wood;
5 – Buxton Heath; 6 – Cley Marshes;
7 – Cockshoot Broad; 8 – East Winch
Common; 9 – East Wretham Heath;
10 – Foxley Wood; 11 – Hethel Old Thorn;
12 – Hickling Broad; 13 – Holkham Fen;
14 – Hoe Rough; 15 – Holme Dunes;
16 – Holt Lowes; 17 – Honeypot Wood;
18 – Lolly Moor; 19 – Lower Wood,
Ashwellthorpe; 20 – Martham Broad;
21 – Narborough Railway Line; 22 – New
Buckenham Common; 23 – Ranworth
Broad; 24 – Ringstead Downs;
25 – Roydon Common and Grimston
Warren; 26 – Salthouse Marshes;
27 – Scarning Fen; 28 – Sparham Pools;
29 – Stanley Carrs; 30 – Swangey Fen;
31 – Syderstone Common; 32 – Thetford
Heath; 33 – Thompson Common;
34 – Thorpe Marshes; 35 – Thursford
Wood; 36 – Upton Broad and Marshes;
37 – Wayland Wood; 38 – Weeting Heath

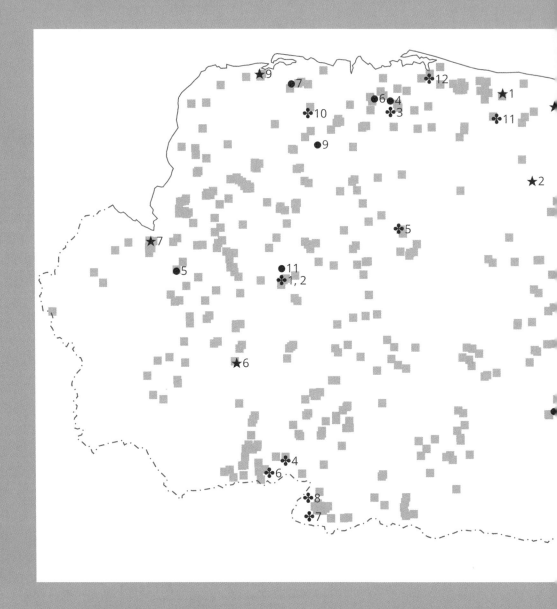

*Map 3* **Protection of historic sites**
Map showing protection of historic sites by government
designation and voluntary trusts.

★ National Trust

● Norfolk Archaeological Trust

✤ English Heritage

▪ Scheduled Ancient Monument

★5

●2

✤15

★3

✤16

✤14

●1

✤13

0    10    20 km

# Abbreviations

| | |
|---|---|
| ADAS | Agricultural Development Advisory Service |
| AONB | Area of Outstanding Natural Beauty |
| BL | British Library |
| CLA | Country Landowners' Association |
| CPRE | Council for the Protection of Rural England |
| DoE | Department of the Environment |
| ESA | Environmentally Sensitive Areas |
| FWAG | Farming and Wildlife Advisory Group |
| MAFF | Ministry of Agriculture, Fisheries and Food |
| MARS | Monuments at Risk Survey |
| NAT | Norfolk Archaeological Trust |
| NCC | Nature Conservancy Council |
| NFU | National Farmers' Union |
| NMMP | Norfolk Monuments Management Project |
| NNAS | Norfolk and Norwich Archaeological Society |
| NNNS | Norfolk and Norwich Naturalists' Society |
| NNT | Norfolk Naturalists' Trust |
| NRO | Norfolk Record Office |
| NWT | Norfolk Wildlife Trust |
| PP | Parliamentary Papers |
| RCAHME | Royal Commission on Ancient and Historical Monuments in England |
| RSPB | Royal Society for the Protection of Birds |
| SPA | Specially Protected Area |
| SPAB | Society for the Protection of Ancient Buildings |
| SPNR | Society for the Promotion of Nature Reserves |
| SSSI | Site of Special Scientific Interest |
| TNA | The National Archives |
| TNNNS | Transactions of the Norfolk and Norwich Naturalist Society |

# The Conservation Movement in Norfolk

A HISTORY

# Introduction

'Rare and beautiful Norfolk,' as John Sell Cotman called it in 1841, is undoubtedly less rare and beautiful than it was, but we have some grounds for hope. An increasing number of people care about the county, its buildings and its landscape.[1]

The landscape of Norfolk is one of the most diverse in the British Isles. While the sandy heaths of Breckland record some of the greatest daily extremes of temperature, the watery landscapes of the Broads and Fens provide habitats for some of our rarest species, such as swallowtail butterflies and bitterns, as well as rich feeding grounds for visiting waders. The salt marshes and pebble spits of the north Norfolk coast are home to some of the largest tern colonies in Britain, while the Halvergate marshes are the largest area of grazed grassland, outside Somerset, in England. The county as a whole, once the most prosperous and populous in the country, is rich in archaeology and landscapes dating back to prehistoric times, with the earliest evidence for man outside Africa recently discovered on the east-facing beach at Happisburgh. Across the county are areas of woodland, heath, historic parklands and commons. As a result of a growing appreciation of this diverse, but fragile, heritage the county now contains ten National Nature Reserves, four Special Protection Areas for birds, seven internationally important 'Ramsar' wetlands, over 430 Scheduled Ancient Monuments and 11,000 listed buildings.[2]

The history of the conservation movement since its early beginnings in the nineteenth century is not just a story of the preservation of natural landscapes, significant historical buildings and archaeological sites; it is more about changing social attitudes and priorities. While nineteenth-century landlords were primarily concerned with the conservation of their game birds to the exclusion of others, later generations have emphasised access to natural and cultural sites for the enjoyment of all. This in itself can lead to conflict between those who wish to preserve areas for research purposes, from which the general public are excluded, and those who advocate open access. Between these two extremes are many gradations, often in the past distinguished by class divisions. In the late nineteenth century, for instance, these could be characterised as 'the battue of the plutocrats, the botanizing and ramblings of the middle class, often armed with cameras, and the hiking of the working class'.[3] By the early twentieth century the extension of the rail network and the advent of the motor car meant that there were conflicts of interest between those who had recently moved to their 'rural idyll' and those wishing to build more houses and join them. What is noticeable through all these arguments is that the views of the country people, the majority of whom worked long hours for low wages and lived in overcrowded damp cottages, were never sought. They remained 'idealised, but neglected' and the arguments were between those wishing to partake in conflicting recreational activities.[4]

The development of interest in conservation in its many forms can be linked to the gradual increase in and widening of access to leisure time. Before 1800 the privilege of leisure was almost exclusively the preserve of the landed classes. They were responsible for laying out country parks and for planting them with trees for aesthetic and economic reasons, as well as to provide cover for foxes and game birds. These private worlds would then be surrounded with high walls and protected with man traps and spring guns. The enjoyment of the countryside involved keeping other people out.

As the eighteenth century progressed so did the nation's wealth. Norwich was one of England's most prosperous cities and the countryside was the home of wealthy landowners, although a wider section of the population was able to enjoy some leisure. The traditional landed families were joined by those who had made money in trade, the colonies and industry. The middle class did not aspire to own land, but they came to enjoy various aspects of the countryside. The mid-eighteenth century saw a flourishing body of amateur botanists in Norwich, many of whom were doctors or clergymen. Later in the century the romantic poets and the painters of the 'Norwich School' were contributing in a different way to interest in the countryside. Their works appealed to a wide audience who, using the newly developing toll roads, flocked to the areas their work made famous. Wild landscapes which in the past had been seen as places to be tamed and brought into 'usefulness' were now admired for their natural beauty. This new leisured class, following in the footsteps of the poets, would walk long distances among mountains and waterfalls and along cliffed coasts to sketch, paint and try their hands at versifying.

Some would take a more serious interest in their surroundings. While the sons of the aristocracy were travelling to the south to visit the roots of civilisation in Greece and Italy, those less wealthy and without the luxury of long periods of leisure were studying the plants and antiquities nearer home. County volumes were being produced describing local sites, ruins and flora. Norwich painters were producing volumes of etchings depicting the antiquities of the county. Gentlemen would venture forth to open up burial mounds and unearth Roman villas. County archaeological societies were founded.

Others were more interested in the natural world. Botanising and producing plant lists became popular pursuits alongside bird watching and egg collecting. Sadly, though, to prove the existence of a species so that it could be included on a bird list a specimen had to be produced, thus hastening the extinction of some rare species. While the field sports of the aristocrats and gentry were exclusively enjoyed by the landed classes, others could enjoy a day rambling along the hedgerows and beaches looking for as yet unrecorded plants, fungi and mosses.

As transport became easier, firstly with the railways and later the bicycle, and in the twentieth century with the bus, coach and private car, participation in these pursuits became more general. The invention of the camera allowed for yet another hobby to develop. Not only were landscapes, castles, churches, plants and animals suitable subjects for pictures, but also the 'quaint' in the countryside, which was unfamiliar to many of these travellers from the towns.

As travel became universal it also became cheaper. Trains and bicycles made hiking and camping possible and demands for access to land, particularly within easy reach of major industrial centres, increased. Conflicts between various interest groups ensued. The serious researchers wanted areas protected because of their natural or cultural interest, while the ramblers wanted open access.

The last years of the twentieth century saw new areas of conflict as modern farming methods were seen as threats to the countryside, leading to the development of government incentives to encourage 'sustainable agriculture' through a variety of environmental stewardship schemes, the most important of which were pioneered in the Broads.

Norfolk has many firsts in the history of conservation which have provided models for other parts of the country. It is the aim of this book not simply to chronicle the gradual development of an interest in conservation, from its origins in the researchers of the eighteenth century to the often pioneering work of the twentieth in conserving what is worth protecting in Norfolk, but also to chart the changing attitudes and social developments which have made this possible.

1  D. Dymond (1985) *The Norfolk landscape*. London, Hodder and Stoughton, 259.
2  Norfolk County Council (1994) *Norfolk countryside conservation strategy*. Norwich, NCC, 4. The main focus of this book is on rural conservation. Hence, there is little discussion of the great medieval city of Norwich with its cathedral – one of the finest Romanesque buildings in Britain – or Kings Lynn and Great Yarmouth, both with an important built heritage. Where mention is made of urban examples, it is when they represent milestones in the legislative process.
3  P. Lowe (1989) 'The rural idyll defended: from preservation to conservation', in G.E. Mingay (ed.), *The rural idyll*. London, Routledge, 117.
4  Lowe 1989, 117.

# 1

## The beginnings of the conservation movement

*The pioneering botanists of the Norwich Botanical Society*

The conservation movement has been built up on the researches of numerous individuals who painstakingly produced evidence of the rich diversity of our natural and cultural heritage which we have come to believe is worth preserving. To form the basis of such a movement these studies must not consist simply of the disconnected pursuits of isolated individuals but be the product of the individuals linked as groups that are able to share knowledge and begin to influence others. These beginnings can be traced back to the seventeenth century, when books began to be published and knowledge shared. The intellectual curiosity given freedom by the Renaissance, and coupled with advances in printing, encouraged the study of the natural and ancient world to develop and the results of research to be circulated. This was part of the general awakening of interest in scientific investigation reflected in the founding of the Royal Society in London in 1660. Although it met and was based in the capital its influence spread to the provinces, encouraging the publication of scientific books. It gave the study of such subjects as zoology and botany a social standing and respectability.

Sir Thomas Browne (1605-1682) is a typical product of this new curiosity. Having trained as a doctor in England and Europe he settled in Norwich in 1637,

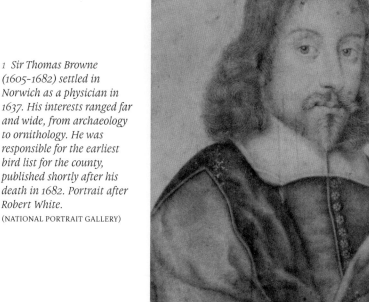

*1 Sir Thomas Browne (1605-1682) settled in Norwich as a physician in 1637. His interests ranged far and wide, from archaeology to ornithology. He was responsible for the earliest bird list for the county, published shortly after his death in 1682. Portrait after Robert White.*
(NATIONAL PORTRAIT GALLERY)

where he attended the wealthy citizens and gentry on their sick beds. By the time of his death, however, he was a writer of international repute. His output not only covered religious subjects but his surroundings, including natural history and archaeology, in which he took a keen interest. His enquiring mind and systematic observations led him into such topics as the diseases associated with the climate of Iceland, the results of imprisoning a viper, a mole and a toad together under glass, and the workings of the human eyelid.[i] Unlike many of his contemporaries, he was convinced that migration, not hibernation, accounted for the absence of certain species in the winter. A prolific essayist, his 'Discourse on the Spechral Urns found in Norfolk' was published in 1658, while at the same time he was collecting stuffed birds and their eggs. His 'Account of the birds found in Norfolk', published after his death in 1682, is the earliest attempt at a species list for the county. The diarist John Evelyn visited him in 1671 and was shown his collection of eggs, 'that country being frequented, as he said, by

*2  Sir James Smith (1753-1817), botanist and founder of the Linnean Society, was born in Norwich and moved back there in 1797 where, over the next thirty years, he wrote the first four volumes of the* English Flora. *He is shown here studying one of the herbaria which formed the reference works for his writings. Portrait by John Rising.*

several kinds which seldom or never go further into the land, such as cranes, storks, eagles and a variety of water fowl'. His scientific curiosity led him to investigate why glow worms glowed and how the bittern produced its strange boom.[2] He found in the flourishing city of Norwich an intelligentsia of like-minded people with whom he could share his enthusiasm.

Nationally, a few lone antiquaries such as John Leland (1503-1552), William Camden (1551-1623) and Sir William Dugdale (1605-1686) were beginning to recognise the value and interest of monuments of the past. At the same time Shakespeare's plays increased an awareness of national history. The opening up of the classical world increased interest both in archaeology and in the origins of a 'British' civilisation. The first British book devoted to archaeological remains,

*Monumenta Britannica*, was written by John Aubrey (1626-1697) and published in 1674. At a slightly later date the Lincolnshire doctor and later priest, William Stukeley (1687-1765), was publishing drawings and descriptions of English antiquities and buildings. He was a founder of the Society of Antiquaries (1707) and its secretary for the first nine years of its existence.

Norwich was at the centre of a productive countryside, much of which was in the hands of the gentry. By the late seventeenth century many were taking a great interest in the improvement of agriculture on their estates, and coupled with this was an interest in the natural as well as the cultivated landscape. Some landlords were both patrons and individual practitioners of the new sciences. One such protégée was Benjamin Stillingfleet (1702-1771), who became tutor to the young William Windham of Felbrigg Hall in north Norfolk. There he cultivated in his pupil an interest in the natural world, and together they studied the plants of the neighbourhood. Here he met another son of a Norfolk landowner, Robert Marsham, who shared with him an interest in botany.[3] Together they began keeping records of weather and temperature, and of the dates when different species of trees came into leaf and migrating birds arrived. By 1736 Marsham was recording tables of the 'Indications of Spring', which covered twenty-six occurrences that he thought heralded the coming of spring – records which he kept for a further sixty years.[4] When, in 1737, Stillingfleet accompanied William on the Grand Tour, they explored the Mer de Glace in the valley of Chamounix and, together with Dr Richard Pococke, wrote a geographical paper on their findings. On their return, Stillingfleet was given a pension by the Windham family and moved away from Norfolk. However, his friendship with Marsham remained and he spent long periods with him at Stratton Strawless, where he helped him keep his Indications of Spring in great detail.

Meanwhile Robert Marsham inherited the family estate at Stratton Strawless. Much of it was poor gravelly land that he proposed planting with trees. He took personal responsibility for the planting and pruning of his trees and carried out a variety of experiments to encourage their growth which he monitored by taking annual measurements. He then submitted his findings to the Royal Society. Several papers of his were published in their *Transactions* and he was elected a fellow in 1780. His contribution to science was to prove that, with proper cultivation, all types of trees could be grown on poor soils.

English botanists had been greatly inspired and excited by the publication in 1735 of Carl Linnaeus' *Systema Natura*, a book in which he proposed the classification of plants on a binary system, firstly by species and then by genus. His ideas were further developed in *Species Plantarum*, published in 1753. Stillingfleet's interest in botany increased and in 1759 he published a translation of Linnaeus' work as well as an essay of his own entitled 'Observation on grasses', the first work in English to follow the Linnaean system of classification.[5]

Throughout most of the eighteenth century Norwich remained a prosperous city. Its wealth was generated by serving its productive agricultural hinterland and by the manufacture of cloth. It supported an expanding and active cultural and intellectual 'middle class', many of whom were associated with the free-thinking dissenting movement. The prominent Norwich botanist James Smith (see below), founder of the Linnean Society, was a unitarian who worshipped at the Octagon chapel. Simon Wilkins, who edited the works of Sir Thomas Browne, was a founder member of the Literary Institution and a prominent baptist. Public circulating libraries proliferated and literary and scientific societies were founded very much in the tradition of the lunar societies to be found in the new industrial cities. The United Friars Society, for instance, was founded in 1785 and its members included both shopkeepers and professional men who met to discuss topical scientific subjects.[6]

The city was also famous for its formal gardens and its horticulturists. A Natural History Society was established in Norwich in 1747 by William Arderon, who had been elected a member of the Royal Society two years earlier. It provided a forum for the acquisition and dissemination of knowledge about flora and fauna.[7] It was still in existence in 1804, when its members were described as being of humble origins, weavers or tailors, who 'amused themselves in herborising in the country'. They would then attempt to identify their findings from the illustrations in 'quaint old herbals'.[8] 'Their trade journeys among their fellow workers took them beyond the confines of the city ... the countryside for twenty miles around Norwich being full of looms', and provided ample opportunity for plant collecting. The gradual acceptance of the Linnean system of classification acted as an impetus to their work and this rather patronising description underestimated the important research carried out by many of the members. John Pitchforth, a surgeon of the city, specialised in mints and sedges. The herbarium of a fellow surgeon, William Skrimshire of Wisbech, is preserved in Wisbech museum. A third surgeon was James Crowe, who collected cuttings from Norfolk willows, which he then planted in his garden at Lakenham, just outside the city. Dr Frederick Long of Wells studied the plants in his area and his herbarium is in the Castle Museum in Norwich. He was the father of Sydney Long, of whom more later.

Among the leading members of the Society was Mr Rose, apothecary (1707-1792), living in Tombland. He had written, with the Reverend Henry Bryant, *Elements of Botany*, which was a translation of Linnaeus' work and contained an appendix listing some Norfolk and Suffolk plants discovered by other Norwich enthusiasts. In 1779 Rose became blind and gave up his apothecary business, although he still retained his botanical interests. Henry Bryant, a distinguished mathematician, was an assistant at St Peter Mancroft before moving to his own parishes in Heydon, Colby and, finally, Langham. He is said to have begun the study of botany after the death of his wife. Another member of this group was John Pitchford, a surgeon who settled in Norwich in 1769. His particular interest, as noted above, was sedges and mints; in 1790 he wrote that he was 'mint-mad'. He died in 1803. In the 1770s a regular visitor to Mr Rose and his library was James Smith, son of a woollen draper in Gentleman's Walk. In later years Smith wrote 'In my young time [the 1770s] this circle [of Norwich botanists] was enriched by the possession of Mr Rose, Mr Bryant, and Mr Pitchford and was often favoured with the society of the learned and amiable Mr Stillingfleet, and the correspondence of Hudson, and they may altogether be considered the founders of Linnean botany in England'.[9] James' interest in botany grew and although his father had intended him for the family business he agreed that he should study medicine (the only course in which botany was included). In 1781 he went to Edinburgh University and from there to London, where he remained in contact with the most eminent botanists of the day, including Sir Joseph Banks. After the death of Linnaeus both his plant collection and library were sold, and James Smith was the purchaser. In 1785 he was made a Fellow of the Royal Society at the time that Sir Joseph Banks was president. In 1787, with the collection housed in Paradise Row, Chelsea, Smith organised a series of meetings there which in 1788 resulted in the founding of the Linnean Society, now based at Burlington House, Piccadilly, where it is the oldest botanical society continuing in existence.[10]

In 1797 Smith married and moved back to Norwich, bringing the Linnean collection with him. This ensured a constant stream of visitors who wanted to use this reference collection and so the circle of Norwich botanists was enriched by discussions with others from further afield. During the following thirty years Smith wrote the first four volumes of the *English Flora* (for which James Crowe's Lakenham willows formed the basis of the willow section) and between 1790 and 1814 the text for *English Botany*.

One of Smith's many botanist friends in Norfolk was Dawson Turner (1775–1855), a banker from Yarmouth. Between 1790 and 1793 Turner was sent to a school run by the Reverend Robert Forby of Fincham, himself a botanist, and together they went on 'botanical rambles' which kindled Turner's interest in the subject. In the eighteenth century Great Yarmouth was a flourishing port and contained, like Norwich, an enthusiastic band of botanists, including the eminent Victorian surgeon Sir James Paget and his brother, the authors of *A sketch of the natural history of the Yarmouth district*, published in 1834. It represented the first attempt to produce a comprehensive flora and fauna of the region with a brief indicator of how common each species was. However, the section on birds was written very much from the point of view of a collector. In this he wrote 'probably no neighbourhood has been investigated so completely as this, which has had the good fortune to have been for nearly a century, the constant stage for the action of some enquiring mind'. He went on to list several eighteenth-century inhabitants of Yarmouth who were well respected for their studies. It was this circle of botanists that Turner entered in the 1790s. His particular areas of study were mosses and seaweeds. Living by the Norfolk coast, he was able to study seaweeds in their fresh state rather than relying on dried specimens. Classification also involved the use of microscopes to identify minute flowers, and so detailed drawings made through a microscope were an important aid to classification. In 1807 Turner embarked on the ambitious task of producing a study of seaweeds for which he relied on the artistic skills of a fellow enthusiast, the Norfolk-born William Hooker. Hooker's first interest was horticulture, but he soon developed his drawing skills. He had close links with the Norwich School of artists and was responsible for most of the drawings in Turner's great four-volume work on seaweeds, entitled *Fuci* and finally completed in 1819. By this date Hooker had married Turner's daughter and in later years left Norfolk,

3 *Dawson Turner (1775-1850), a Yarmouth banker and keen antiquarian and naturalist responsible for a major study of seaweeds illustrated by the Norwich-born William Hooker, who later became Director of Kew Gardens. His antiquarian interest led him to collect manuscripts and seals as well as to illustrate his own copy of Blomefield's* History of Norfolk. *He was also instrumental in ensuring the publication of some of Kirkpatrick's antiquarian works. Drawing by J.P. Davies, 1816.*

J.P.Davis delⁿ 1816.                    Printed by Graf & Soret.

DAWSON TURNER ESQᵗ

becoming from 1841 to 1865 director of Kew Gardens. Turner himself followed Smith as president of the Linnaean Society from 1828 to 1833.[11]

Smith and his wife made their home in Surrey Street, which was designed by the Norwich architect Thomas Ivory and consisted of large fashionable three-storey brick houses with elegant porches and large gardens reminiscent of the style Smith was used to in London. On the death of Smith's widow, Joseph Geldart took over the Surrey Street house. Not surprisingly, the garden was full of unusual plants, which probably helped fire Joseph's son, Herbert Decimus,

4 *Surrey Street in Norwich was a fashionable development designed by Thomas Ivory in the 1770s. This was the home of not only James Smith but the late nineteenth-century botanist Herbert Geldart.*

5 *Opposite: Pages from the herbaria compiled by some of the early Norfolk botanists now held in the Norwich Castle Museum. Smith's volume contains a wide variety of specimens from across Europe, while the specimens in Paget's (1832) are meticulously labelled, as are those in the Norfolk Botanical Society volumes (1858).*

with an interest in botany. Herbert was to become one of Norfolk's finest late nineteenth-century botanists, an enthusiastic member of the newly founded Norfolk and Norwich Naturalist Society and a contributor to its journal. In 1901 he was largely responsible for the Natural History section in the first volume of the *Victoria County History* for Norfolk, which contained detailed bird, flora and fauna lists for the county. He was well known for the importance of his collections, though many of these were put together by gathering material from earlier collectors.

These early botanists were primarily interested in collecting, classifying and exchanging specimens to enhance their own collections and create their own herbaria, several of which, including that of J.D. Salmon (1802–1859), are now in Norwich Castle Museum. Salmon lived in Thetford and worked in the family

brewery. His interests were wide, covering birds and insects as well as plants, and his meticulously kept herbaria include many plants not now found in Breckland. He also kept in contact with gamekeepers and bought bird specimens for the newly founded museum, including the last great bustard, which was shot in South Acre. It remained at the Castle Museum until it became so eaten by insects that it had to be destroyed. The only remaining example in the county may well be that at Holkham Hall. These enthusiasts were in frequent and detailed correspondence with each other, and those living in both Norwich and Yarmouth would have formed tight networks which also stretched out across the county. The prosperity of both town and country in the eighteenth century allowed many to have the leisure to pursue their interests in the rich intellectual, independent and enquiring atmosphere of these two major urban centres. Scouring fields, hedgerows, heaths, coasts, cliffs and chalk pits for plants to classify and collect in a countryside that was fast changing as a result of agricultural progress, their ranks included urban doctors, lawyers and shopkeepers as well as rural squires. Peering through their microscopes to identify the tiny variations within species, they came to appreciate the intricate wonders of nature. Among the herbaria which have found their way into Norwich Castle Museum is that of James Paget, dating from the 1830s. It is carefully labelled with the site from which each plant was taken. A collection put together by James Smith contains plants from his garden as well as some exchanged with fellow botanists from as far afield as Switzerland. The herbarium of Norwich Botanical Society was given to the museum in 1858 by Mrs E. Bleakley, but unfortunately the locations from which the plants were taken are rarely given.

The first county flora to be published was that written by the Reverend Kirby Trimmer in 1866. To do this he relied on his own catalogues made when he was curate, firstly at Stanhoe, in the north-west of the county, and then at Crostwick, to the north of Norwich, as well as help from fellow botanists, including John Salmon and Admiral Nelson's sister Susanna, who sent him many coastal plants. A second *Flora*, by W. Nicholson (1877-1925), was published in 1913. On a much more limited scale the Reverend Galpin's *Flowering plants and birds of Harleston*, written over a five-year period and published in 1888, was a fine example of meticulous work on a small area. Thus 'following the wonderful age of discovery, from about 1780 to 1830, botanical research in the county moved progressively forward in the nineteenth century'.[12] The work of the botanists marked the beginning of a new and genuine interest in the diversity of the natural world in which Norfolk was already an important player and which was to provide the bedrock without which the conservation movement could not begin.

## The early ornithologists

Just as the botanists were spurred on by a desire to collect, so were the ornithologists, collecting both eggs and birds to add to their glass cases of specimens. By the nineteenth century Norfolk was recognised as one of the richest ornithological districts in Britain. Its long and varied coastline projecting into the North Sea was visited by many migratory birds, and the range of landscapes, including the Broads, fens, heath, woodland and farmland, meant that it supported a great number of species.

Techniques of taxidermy improved greatly through the nineteenth century, thus fuelling the fashion for displays of stuffed birds. Indeed, for a species to be added to the county bird lists of the time, a 'specimen' had to be produced. This could lead to problems if the provenance of the specimen was unclear. The Wilson's Petrel, for instance, which had appeared on the 1864 list, was removed in 1883 because 'the single specimen said to have been killed at Salthouse in 1839, would seem from later investigation to have reached Norfolk as a skin'.[13] However, the dangers of this increasing interest in collecting were already becoming recognised. As early as 1838 the Norfolk ornithologist Richard Pigott wrote a letter to *The Naturalist* published under the headline 'Impropriety of Wantonly Shooting Birds' – the earliest call for moderation to be accorded such prominence.[14]

The earliest known published bird list for Norfolk is that of 1682 by Sir Thomas Browne. It was not until 1815 that this was superseded by John Hunt's unfinished collection of notes and engravings entitled *British Ornithology*. The study of natural history was very much the preserve of the local clergy. In 1826 the Reverend R. Sheppard and the Reverend W. Whitear published an article in the Linnean Society Transactions entitled 'A Catalogue of the Norfolk and Suffolk birds with remarks' which for the first time contained a complete list of the birds of both counties. The Reverend Richard Lubbock , rector of the south Norfolk parish of Eccles from 1837 to 1876, was a member of the Committee of Norwich Museum from 1831 and published *Observations of the fauna of Norfolk and more particularly of the district of the Broads* in 1845. In it he wrote 'our marshes are more and more improved and drained for the sake of patronage; and under the plea of gathering lapwings' eggs almost all birds which remain in the summer have their nests regularly plundered'. Gurney and Fisher's 'Account of the birds found in Norfolk', published in the *Zoologist* of 1846, not only listed 277 species but described the environmental changes that were affecting bird numbers. By 1864 the list numbered 293. Records of the shooting of several additional species in the *Transactions of the Norfolk Naturalist Society* over the next twenty years led to the addition of eleven new species by 1883, although eleven were also removed from the list because of inaccurate identifications, so the number remained the same. The draining of marshes, the enclosure of heaths and the extension of agriculture were already recognised as dangers to the diversity of bird life.[15]

The first major work on Norfolk birds to be more than a list was published in 1866. It was the two-volume *Birds of Norfolk* by Henry Stevenson, printer, bookseller, stationer and the publisher of the *Norfolk Chronicle*. As distinct from the books and articles cited above, it became widely available and remained a valuable reference book. Unlike a modern bird book, it was almost entirely unillustrated. A frontispiece to Volume 1 showed a broadland scene with a bittern and coots in the foreground, while the frontispiece to Volume 2 was the only illustration of a bird and this was of the already extinct great bustard. Further on in the volume was a view across the marshes towards Yarmouth. This choice of subject demonstrates the area of the county considered to be of greatest interest to the ornithologist. Each entry is supported by a record of the provenanced specimens reported to the author and followed by notes on the habits of the bird. The importance of relying on specimens which had been shot and preserved for evidence of sightings is obvious throughout the book. However, the lack of illustrations must have limited its usefulness for identifying species. A collector and wildfowler himself, whose chief pleasure was in shooting snipe, Stevenson soon became aware of the dangers to the survival of some species that this pursuit was imposing. In his presidential address in 1872 to the recently formed Norfolk and Norwich Naturalists' Society he warned of the destruction of wildlife that was going on. In the first half of the century 600 to 700 lapwing, redshank and greeve eggs per week were sent from Yarmouth to the London market. Avocet eggs from Salthouse were used for cooking. As more land was drained their nests became more vulnerable and the birds less numerous 'and the eggs sought for with still greater avidity, extinction becomes an inevitable result'. 'In one season upwards of seventy eggs of the beautiful bearded tit were taken at Surlingham. Though abundant there twenty years ago, this bird is now rarely seen.'[16] As early as 1845 Lubbock wrote that early in the season eggs of lapwings, redshanks, greeves and tern could fetch eighteen pence (15p) each. Yet he himself was a sportsman, renting shooting in the Broads and killing eleven bittern in one season.[17]

Egg collecting was therefore seen as a major reason for the reduction in the number of birds and was a concern to serious ornithologists. The adoption of horse hoeing had facilitated the discovery of the eggs of ground-nesting birds, which could be sold for a high price, among the spring corn. Collecting had led by 1883 to the extermination of the black-tailed godwit, the black tern and the avocet, while there were fears for the bearded tit 'in almost their last remaining British nesting place'.[18]

It was not only egg collecting but the increasing interest in collecting stuffed birds which went with the improving techniques of taxidermy which threatened the rare species. The fine collection at Holkham, collected between 1850 and 1915, included 106 specimens. It included most of the common coastal, hedgerow and field species, mainly shot in the vicinity of Holkham. A white-tailed eagle, captured at nearby Cockthorpe in 1850, was kept in captivity until it 'became savage', before being poisoned and stuffed. A Sabines gull was 'captured in the shore nets on the Wells Sands' in 1892 and a dotterel was 'killed against telephone wires on the Warham Road' in 1897. A unique item was the great bustard, which was said to have been given to the children of Mr Wylie of Peterstone brickyards in the 1860s as a play thing, but was rescued by Colonel Fielden and added to the collection in 1889. It was thought to have come from the Sedgeford area.[19] The birds were exhibited in the audit room and in 1941 the collection was recognised as being of 'national significance'.[20] Although still in existence, they are no longer on public display.

With the improvements in the design of the breech-loading shotgun, the mid-nineteenth century saw the beginning of a huge expansion of interest in

*The Birds of Norfolk.*

J.Wolf.& J.Jury.lith.  M.& N.Hanhart.imp

"BARGATE" SURLINGHAM BROAD.

*The Birds of Norfolk*

M.& N.Hanhart lith.

BREYDON "FLATS" NEAR YARMOUTH.

6 *Illustrations from Stevenson's* Birds of Norfolk *(1870), showing the distinctive Norfolk landscapes of particular interest to the ornithologists of the time: Breydon Water and Surlingham Broad, both in Broadland, and Thetford Warren in Breckland (opposite).*

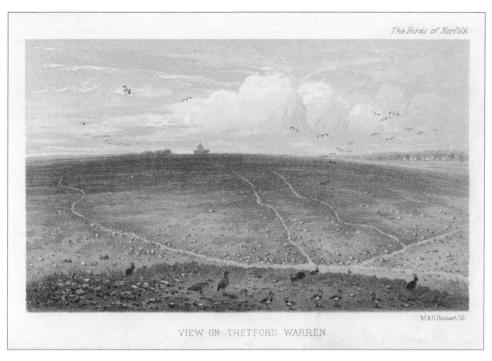

VIEW ON THETFORD WARREN.

GREAT BUSTARD

*7 The great bustard, as illustrated as the frontispiece to* Birds of Norfolk *was already extinct by this date.*

field sports, particularly pheasant and partridge shooting. The heyday of the great Norfolk shooting estates and the popularity of the *battue*, whereby the birds were driven up into the air by beaters for the guns to shoot, lasted until after the First World War. At Holkham the annual 'bag' rose from 3,252 partridges and 1,443 pheasants in 1853-4 to 4,599 partridges and 4,149 pheasants in 1900-1901, with even greater increases on the Sandringham, Felbrigg and Blickling estates.[21] It was not so much the killing of these carefully reared and guarded birds that was a threat to wildlife but the activities of gamekeepers in destroying their predators, such as the larger birds of prey. As White's *Directory* of 1883 predicted, 'No falcon, hawk, harrier or buzzard can long expect to escape the doom of its race in a strictly game-preserving district like the county of Norfolk.' Kestrels and sparrowhawks were still to be found in the 1880s and nests of 'all three harriers are occasionally found in the neighbourhood of the Broads'. However, the smaller birds, such as thrushes, blackbirds, finches, buntings and larks, benefited from the control of the birds of prey.[22] Of greater significance, however, were the activities of the punt gunners on the waterways of the Broads and fens. Punt guns were fowling pieces notorious for their massive 'overkill'. One Norfolk exponent of this sport was said to have killed 603 knot, nine redshank and five dunlin as the result of just two shots at a range of eighty yards.[23]

## The early antiquaries

At the same time as the botanists and ornithologists were busy collecting and classifying their specimens, another group of collectors was also at work. Interest in the cultural heritage was increasing and it was the early antiquaries who, like the naturalists, paved the way for the concern over conservation, in this case of historic buildings and archeological sites. Many of the young men who came back from the grand tour, often with classical artefacts with which to adorn their country mansion houses, were fired with an interest in the past of their own homeland. This included both Roman and pre-Roman remains, as well as medieval ruins such as castles and abbeys. Some, such as the Lee-Warners at Walsingham, were fortunate enough to have a genuine abbey ruin within their park which they could incorporate into the landscaping. These enthusiasts were busy collecting not only artefacts but also documents with which to fill their libraries, alongside making a record of historic sites.

By the early eighteenth century a small group of antiquarians was collecting and exchanging information across the county. Thomas Tanner (1674-1735) arrived in Norfolk from Queen's College Oxford. He came to Norfolk as chancellor of the diocese and private chaplain to the bishop of Norwich in 1698, and collected folios of manuscripts before he moved away from the county in 1731. Of a similar date was Peter Le Neve (1661-1729) of Witchingham, who, from 1707 to 1724, was the first president of the Society of Antiquaries. He collected manuscripts particularly relating to heraldry as well as transcribing and annotating Bishop Edward Reynold's Norfolk Visitation of Norfolk parishes in 1664. A third member of this early group was Thomas Martin (1697-1771), a lawyer from Thetford who settled in Palgrave and took over Le Neve's collection when he died. Benjamin Mackerell (d. 1738) was an assistant to Le Neve and the librarian of Norwich Public Library, which he catalogued. He also published a history of Kings Lynn in 1738. Perhaps the most meticulous antiquarian of this group was John Kirkpatrick (1686-1728), a linen merchant in Norwich who became, in 1726, the treasurer of the Great Hospital. His early death meant that in spite of all his work collecting and transcribing documents, as well as his careful observations and sketches of medieval buildings, none of his work was published during his lifetime.[24] In 1845 Dawson Turner published Kirkpatrick's *History of the Religious Orders of Norwich* and in 1889 the Archaeological Society published his *Streets and Lanes of Norwich*, both of which had survived as manuscripts. Many of Kirkpatrick's original drawings and notes are in the Norfolk Record Office. In 1723 his brother, Thomas, published a large engraving of the north-east prospect of Norwich which John was responsible for selling. Again, this is a detailed and closely observed work. Dawson Turner described him as one of the 'most laborious, learned and useful antiquarians whom Norfolk produced ... an indefatigable searcher into local antiquities who had accumulated copious materials, but his early death prevented him from digesting and publishing them'.[25] In common with other antiquarians of the time, one of his chief interests was in the collection of manuscripts, coins and medals. Henry Ninham described him as 'chief of our city antiquarians',[26] who had made drawings of all the old city gates as well as local antiquities such as the ruined gate of St Benet's Abbey.

Henry Ninham (1793-1874) is best known for his faithful depictions of Norwich's ancient buildings, publishing in 1842 etchings of *Picturesque Antiquities on Norwich and Remnants of Antiquity in Norwich*. In 1864 he etched *Views of the Ancient City Gates of Norwich as they appeared in 1722* from Kirkpatrick's original drawings.[27] These records of contemporary scenes are an invaluable source for modern archaeologists and historians.

Kirkpatrick's work began a tradition carried on by many of the Norwich artists. In 1795 William Wilkins produced a series of watercolour reconstructions of Norwich Castle keep and John Adey Repton undertook detailed elevations of Norwich Cathedral. In a major project of his later life Robert Ladbrooke (1769-1842), one of the founders of the Norwich Society of painters, made drawings of all 700 churches in Norfolk which were then etched for printing by his son. Although the standard of both the drawing and the etching is 'indifferent', they have huge historic value as they show the churches as they were before the work of the Victorian restorers. The fact that he saw that there would be a market for his etchings indicates the increasing level of interest in medieval buildings. Although little of Ladbrooke's art survives, the same cannot be said of John Sell Cotman (1782-1842). Alongside his prolific output of watercolours he found time to produce detailed architectural etchings of the west front of Castle Acre (c.1805) and St Ethelberg's gate, Norwich (1817).

These illustrations were all produced for the growing number of readers eagerly seeking out evidence of their past. Interest was spreading outside a small group of intellectuals to a wider public. The war with France was limiting foreign travel and the romantic movement, fuelled by the historical novel, was catching the popular imagination. For them, Faden included on his map of Norfolk, first published in 1797, 'the remains of Roman roads, and other antiquities'. As the Gothic revival gained support in the nineteenth century professional artists were joined by the wives and daughters of rectors in this work of recording. The nineteenth-century rector Neville-Rolfe organised a group of watercolourists and had a special coach constructed to store their materials, transporting artists from

8 *John Kirkpatrick (1686-1728) was one of the most meticulous of the early antiquarians and his drawings of medieval buildings are of enormous value to modern historians. This one is of the surviving gatehouse at St Benet's Abbey before the removal of the upper floor and the building of the windmill, annotated in 1780 by John Fenn.*

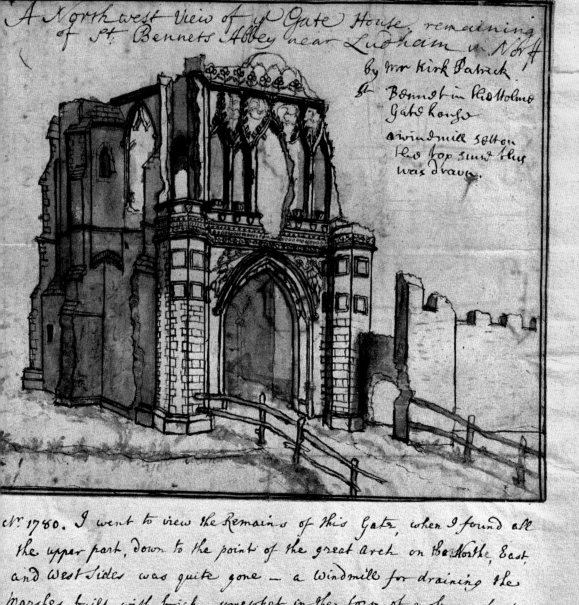

A North west view of ye Gate House, remaining
of St Bennets Abbey near Ludham in Norf

by mr Kirk Patrick

St Bennet in the Holme
Gate house

a windmill set on
the top since this
was drawn.

No 1780. I went to view the Remains of this Gate, when I found all
the upper part, down to the point of the great arch on the North, East,
and West Sides was quite gone — a windmill for draining the
Marshes, built with brick somewhat in the form of a Sugar Loaf
is erected in such a manner, that the West front of the Gate is
now enclosed within it, & a wooden Platform for managing the Sails
lies all round upon the top of the ruins of the gate, to which you
scend by the old stone stairs in the East Front.
This Gate is in the Parish of Horning in Tunsted Hundred.     Jn d Fenn

9 *The west front of Castle Acre Priory, etched by J.S. Cotman c.1805.*

church to church over a period of ten years; the results were used to illustrate his own copy of Blomefield's *History* (see below), now in the Norwich Castle Museum. 'Without their work we would have a far poorer understanding of the iconography of the fifteenth century.'[28]

Unlike the botanisers, who were often clergymen and doctors, but included tradesmen among their number, most of the early antiquaries were clergymen or country gentlemen. Foremost among these was Francis Blomefield (1705-1752), rector of Fersfield,[29] who began his great work, culminating in a parish-by-parish history of Norfolk, in 1739. By his death in 1775 he had completed the first five volumes. It was continued by the Reverend Charles Parkin (1689-1765), rector of Oxborough, who had already been working on some of the west Norfolk parishes. It is unclear how far he had progressed before his death, when the material was bought by William Whittingham, a bookseller of Kings Lynn, who

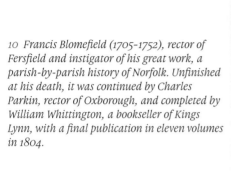

*10 Francis Blomefield (1705-1752), rector of Fersfield and instigator of his great work, a parish-by-parish history of Norfolk. Unfinished at his death, it was continued by Charles Parkin, rector of Oxborough, and completed by William Whittington, a bookseller of Kings Lynn, with a final publication in eleven volumes in 1804.*

published the remaining volumes between 1769 and 1775; a second eleven-volume edition was published in 1804. *An Essay towards a topographical history of Norfolk* set out to provide descriptions of all towns, villages and hamlets with details of all religious buildings, as well as 'castles, seats and manors their present and ancient owners'. Epitaphs and inscriptions in the churches were all included, as well as 'relicks of antiquity'. This information was gathered partly from documentary evidence such as 'ledger-books, registers, records, evidences, deeds, court rolls, and other authentick memorials'[30] and partly from the manuscript collections of men such as Kirkpatrick, Thomas Martin and Thomas Tanner, but also from local sources. In common with other researchers across the country, Blomefield sent out a list of 'queries' to his fellow clergymen. These were printed as a 'letter of enquiry' and consisted of twenty questions covering details about the parish and its manorial history, the church and its chapels, parish charities, the heraldry and genealogy of the landowners and the types of documents surviving in parish chests. Blomefield also asked about archaeological finds and whether there were 'Tumuli, Roman Stations, Ways, Pavements,

Encampments, Trenches, Walls, Fields of Battle or the likes' which could still be seen.[31] He himself travelled widely to copy inscriptions in churches and sift through parish chests and documents in the munument rooms of the gentry and aristocracy. He carried on a voluminous correspondence with his many contacts in his search for information. The work itself was published in individual sections printed on his own press in his rectory and was later assembled into folio volumes. It was financed by his subscribers, who were mostly 'gentlemen in my own way'. It is clear from the emphasis on manorial history and genealogy that Blomefield's book was aimed at the gentry and this is supported by the fact that he offered to include pictures of their country seats if they liked to submit them for etching.

Much of Thomas Martin's and Peter Le Neve's material found its way to John Fenn (1739-1794), the son of a Norwich surgeon who lived in the Cathedral Close. After his father died he moved with his mother to North Elmham and his interest in heraldry is said to have been stimulated by looking at hatchments in North Elmham church. He married in 1766 when he moved to East Dereham and remained there for the rest of his life, acting both as a churchwarden and a director of the local House of Industry. Although he trained as an attorney his main interests were always in the collecting of documents, particularly books and autographs, of which he had 800. His library was said to number 10,000 books. A protégé of Le Neve, he obtained on his death much of his collection, some of which had belonged to Blomefield. This included what was to prove his most important possession: the Paston letters. The comment of a Cambridge friend in 1769, that 'his attentions are so confined to a number of little subjects that he has hardly left room for one great idea', were to prove unfair. He revised and corrected Blomefield's volume on the Hundred of Holt for Whittingham and then embarked on the major task of transcribing the Paston letters. These letters, from a fifteenth-century Norfolk landed family of Oxnead, cover national, local and domestic affairs and have proved a treasure trove to medieval historians. Fenn published the first two volumes in 1787 and, through Horace Walpole, who described him as 'another smatterer in antiquity, but a very good sort of man', he was introduced to the king and dedicated his transcriptions of the letters to him. He was later knighted as a mark of the monarch's appreciation.[32]

The publication of etchings and Blomefield's history all increased interest

11 *John Fenn (1739-1794) (left), famous for his publication of the Paston Letters, moved from North Elmham to East Dereham in 1766, where he owned by far the most prestigious house in the town (below). He was active in local affairs and acted as a church warden and a director of the local House of Industry.*

in visiting historic sites. Castle Acre Priory had been popular from the early eighteenth century and by 1843 there were enough visitors for the tenant farmer to be obliged by the landowner, the earl of Leicester, to show them round. The arrival of the railway in Swaffham increased the site's popularity and by the late 1880s a full-time caretaker was supported by the fee of sixpence paid by each visitor. It was partly excavated at the end of the nineteenth century and the first guide book was published in 1908.[33]

The interest in collecting which so inspired the early naturalists was also to be found among the antiquarians. Foremost among these was Dawson Turner, who, in addition to his botanical activities, was a collector of books and rare manuscripts, particularly if they were autographed. A fashionable pastime was 'extra-illustration', sometimes called 'Grangering' after the man who made it popular. It involved adding information, and particularly drawings, between the leaves of existing reference books to expand the information in them. One of the most significant examples of this is Turner's extra illustration of a copy of Blomefield's Norfolk, which is now in the British Library; Turner's additions resulted in the expansion of the original eleven volumes to 58, together with twelve boxes of deeds and seals. He and his family travelled across the county to draw the many churches, houses and ruined abbeys and castles mentioned by Blomefield, which drawings were then inserted in the appropriate places.[34] A similar project involved the illustration of Henry Swinden's *History of Great Yarmouth* of 1772, now in Norwich Cathedral Library.[35]

## The beginning of county societies

Local societies to encourage investigation into both archaeology and natural history had been founded from the early 1700s. The Spalding (Lincolnshire) Gentleman's Society began in 1710, with William Stukeley as one of its founding members, while that at Wisbech (Cambridgeshire) was founded in 1781. The founder of Spalding's society claimed that 'We deal in arts and sciences and exclude nothing from our conversation but politics, which would throw us all into confusion and disorder.'[36] In common with many others, the Wisbech Literary and Museum Society had its own museum, which survives today. The upkeep of the meeting rooms and the publication of transactions meant that membership of these societies was expensive and therefore often small and elitist.

While much of the botanical, ornithological and antiquarian interest was stimulated by a desire to collect and categorise, it led to an increased concern with and awareness of the diversity to be found within the county, from the smallest insect to the most impressive ruined fortification. Although Norwich had several libraries, it had no museum in which collections could be housed. The Norfolk and Norwich Literary Institution was founded in 1822, with John Harvey, a respected citizen who had been Lord Mayor, as president. The vice-presidents were James Smith and Hudson Gurney MP, Norwich banker and eminent ornithologist, with Simon Wilkins as its secretary and librarian. Wilkins moved to premises on the south side of Haymarket, where the reading room opened in 1823. Discussions of scientific and antiquarian subjects took place and, here, boundaries of class, politics and religious denomination were forgotten in the search for knowledge. It was James Smith who suggested that a collection of objects would be a useful addition to the Institution's collection of books. To fill this gap, the Norfolk and Norwich Museum was founded in 1825 by Smith, who was its first president. He was followed in this position by Dawson Turner. Its first catalogue, published in 1830, opened with the words 'The catalogue will show that the Institution has already acquired a degree of consequence well deserving the patronage of the public and hardly to be expected in an institution only established five years ago.'[37] With such distinguished supporters the museum soon outgrew the Literary Institution and, in 1833, built its own premises in Exchange Street (Norwich's only purpose-built museum, which is now an office equipment shop). The museum was run primarily for the benefit of the subscribers, whose collections formed the bulk of the exhibits, and was not generally open to the public. In 1838 it moved again, to a building in St Andrews Street that has since been demolished, where regular open days were introduced. The museum saw itself as primarily a scientific institution and its collections were mainly of natural history with archaeology and ethnography. However, anything that was offered was accepted, which led to a rather eclectic mix. One of the major donors was Hudson Gurney, president from 1849 to 1890, who had a particular interest in birds of prey. His donation of his huge collection later filled an entire room in the newly opened Castle Museum of the 1890s. Other important gifts were great bustards, extinct in Norfolk from the1830s, given by Jeremiah Colman. Geology and antiquities were also well represented in the early museum. Robert Fitch (1802–1895) ran a chemist's shop in Norwich, but was also an antiquarian who was secretary of the Norfolk and Norwich Archaeological Society for many years. In 1891 he gave his entire collection to the museum and later gave the money for fitting out the Fitch Room at the Castle.

THIS COLLECTION of BRITISH BIRDS WAS FORMED BY EDWARD LOMBE ESQ. OF GREAT MELTON NEAR NORWICH AND WAS PRESENTED TO THE MUSEUM BY MRS. E. P. CLARKE OF WYMONDHAM IN 1873

"LOMBE" COLLECTION OF BIRDS

12  *The Gurney collection of birds, as displayed in the Castle Museum in the 1890s.*

It contained books, seals, rugs, ivories, Saxon and Roman finds, fossils, pottery and porcelain.

By the mid 1880s the building in St Andrews Street was becoming too small and there were problems with damp. Gurney's relation John Gurney of Sprowston Hall was Mayor of Norwich in 1884, when Norwich Castle ceased to be a county jail, and it was he who inspired the City Corporation to buy the castle and convert it into a museum, giving £5,000 towards the purchase. The Norwich architect Edward Boardman was appointed to produce plans for the conversion. Initially the plan was to demolish many of the later prison blocks and retain the castle keep. However, it was soon clear that this would not be large enough and in the final plan the keep was to house only the ethnographical and archaeological collections. The geological, mineralogical and zoological collections, along with the picture gallery, were to be housed in the various wings, with the zoological specimens and the Gurney collection of raptorial birds in the corridors,[38] although they were soon moved to a room of their own. The museum was moved to the castle in 1894 and the old one, with its subscribers, was wound up.

This was a period when the number of municipal museums was increasing. A hundred were set up in the ten years after 1872, stimulated by the success of the Great Exhibition and the opening of the South Kensington Museums in 1857. Many of these museums were newly built behind classical facades, but Nottingham provided a precedent for the conversion of a castle.[39]

The early museum did much to stimulate interest in both natural and cultural history, so it is not surprising that the desire to form county societies grew. The mid-nineteenth century was a time which saw the coming together of isolated individuals who had been pursuing their interests on their own into local county societies (often known as 'Field Clubs') across Britain. This trend manifested in Norfolk with the founding of two distinct societies: the Norfolk and Norwich Archaeological Society (NNAS) in 1846 and the Norfolk and Norwich Naturalists' Society (NNNS) in 1869. As road transport improved during the late eighteenth century and, even more importantly, after 1840, when the railways made travel much easier, the functions of Norwich as a provincial capital multiplied and the practicality of holding regular meetings became a reality. With the founding of county societies interest moved on from the collection and exhibiting of specimens to a concern to protect fragile environments and the opportunity, through the societies, to influence public opinion and thus the future of the countryside. Both societies were able to build on the 'receptive temper of the times' with an increasing middle-class population anxious for self-improvement and with more leisure time.[40]

The 1840s saw the founding of county archaeological societies across the rural, 'squirearchical anglican' counties of England, including Norfolk's neighbours Lincolnshire and Suffolk. Much of the inspiration behind them came from the clergy, who were influenced by the tractarian movement and its encouragement of an interest in the past practices of the church and of its buildings.[41] In common, therefore, with similar county bodies, about two-thirds of the committee members of the Norfolk and Norwich Archaeological Society were clergy and the president was the bishop of Norwich. The idea of founding a society had been mooted by Reverend Munford of East Winch and the antiquarian George Minty of Norwich. The other founding committee members were drawn from the local aristocracy and gentry. Following in the footsteps of Blomefield, much of their interest was in church architecture and Norfolk records. Indeed, one of the aims of the founders was to keep the subscription as low as possible 'so as to bring it within the means of all, and especially with a view of creating a better taste among the class from which churchwardens are drawn'. The preliminary meeting was held at Muskett's shop in the Haymarket in December 1845, with an inaugural meeting in January 1846. Among the early promoters was Dawson Turner, who combined both botanical and antiquarian interests. By 1850 the membership had reached 400. An important element of the early meetings was the exhibition of paintings, coins, rubbings, seals, armour, plans and prehistoric implements, many of which found their way into the museum, of which Dawson Turner was in charge. Excursions also formed an important part of the Society's activities and transport to meetings was normally by train, coupled with brake and waggonette. By the 1880s bicycles and tricycles were ridden by the more active.[42]

While the eighteenth-century antiquarians were mainly interested in medieval and Roman art and archeology there was a move in the nineteenth century towards prehistory, particularly in terms of prehistoric burial mounds and barrow digging. In 1803 Gibson had published details of a mound opened

*13 North Wootton church, as illustrated by Ladbrooke in the early nineteenth century and as it is today; it was rebuilt in 1850-53 by the Victorian Gothic architect Anthony Salvin on much the same footprint.*

at Colney, near Norwich, and in 1848 Lukis described one he had dug at Bircham. Plans of several other excavations and finds survive in Norfolk Museums Service collections, but many of these early excavations have gone unrecorded. At least fifty-five are known to have taken place in the nineteenth century.[43] By the 1840s collectors were seeking out the earliest evidence for man and the national Ethnographical Society, founded in 1843, provided a forum for these researchers. In 1865 John Lubbock, influenced by Darwin's theory of evolution, published *Prehistoric Times*, formalising the Danish archaeologist C.J. Thomsen's now-accepted sequence of old and new stone ages, followed by a bronze and then an iron age.

Probably the most well-known of the clerical members of the NNAS was Augustus Jessopp. He came to Norfolk as head of Norwich Grammar School in 1859 but was rector of Scarning from 1879. He became a member of the Council of the NNAS in 1872 and remained so until the early 1890s. During that time he contributed regularly to *Norfolk Archaeology*, mainly on church history, as well as being the author of several books. He was a great supporter of the Society for the Protection of Ancient Buildings (SPAB), which was founded in 1877 by William Morris in an effort to promote the authentic maintenance of medieval buildings, particularly churches, against the sort of 'restoration' that Morris, Jessopp and others thought 'destructive'. Indeed, concern over the craze for 'restoration', particularly of churches, went back well before Morris. The report of W. Twopenny and architect Edward Blore to the Commission of Woods and Forests in 1846 on

the restoration of ancient buildings belonging to the Crown stated that monuments often suffered from 'injudicious repairs conducted with well meant but ill judged zeal'. The word 'restoration' was apparently often used to cover 'most flagrant destruction' and they drew a distinction between preservation and restoration — 'a distinction little understood by the public'.[44] On this theme Jessopp, in his book *Trials of a Country Parson*, wrote that he wanted 'to raise the voice of warning against a fashion which had become a rage and which was threatening to make a clean sweep of all that was most venerable, most precious, most unapproachably inimitable in the architectural remains of our country'.[45]

*The beginnings of the conservation movement* | 37

He went on to advocate a national register of churches which had escaped the desire to 'restore' and thus survived in their medieval form almost intact. No such register has ever been undertaken, and there is no doubt that activity in Norfolk has resulted in a large number of medieval churches being heavily Victorianised. Some, such as North Wootton, almost entirely rebuilt by Anthony Salvin in 1852–3, West Tofts, where the south chapel, chancel and north aisle were the work of the Pugins, father and son, in the mid-century, and Booton, designed by the rector and friend of Lutyens Reverend Whitwell Elwin and begun in 1875, are hardly recognisable as the buildings illustrated by Ladbrooke a generation before. The Burnham Thorpe restoration was carried out with the enthusiastic support of the Prince of Wales in memory of Nelson, and in the process everything in the church that Nelson might have known was removed. The church reopened on the anniversary of the Battle of the Nile.

There do not seem to have been local objections to church restoration, but there was far more opposition to the work on Norwich Castle. As a result of much concern over the proposal to restore the east, south and north faces in 1834 Blore was asked to survey, report and advise on the best way of proceeding. He reported that the masonry was in a bad state and later repairs had been 'closely assimilated with the original work'. He recommended that the necessary work should be 'judiciously incorporated with the ancient work'. The work was finally carried out by Salvin between 1835 and 1838 and, although faithful to the original design, it was in Bath stone rather than the original Caen.[46] Not everyone was happy. The *Norfolk Chronicle* expressed regret in August 1842 'at the necessity, if any existed, for the adoption of a process which has for ever hidden from human eyes the whole exterior of this celebrated Anglo-Norman keep'.[47]

In 1899 an ambitious national project dedicated to Queen Victoria was launched under the title *The Victoria County History*. The work was overseen by an eminent committee headed by the chancellors of both Oxford and Cambridge, the professor of History at Oxford, Lord Aston, the presidents of the Royal Society and Linnean Society and the director of the National Gallery. Among the less well-known members in 1901 was the Great Yarmouth antiquarian Walter Rye. The local committee for Norfolk was headed by the earl of Leicester and included the heads of the major county families as well as the bishop and dean of Norwich and other clergymen, including Augustus Jessopp. The work would cover every aspect of the county, 'showing the condition of each county at the present day and tracing the domestic history of the English Counties back to earliest times'.[48] Importantly, illustrations were to include 'the beautiful and quaint examples of architecture which through decay and other causes are in danger of disappearing'.[49] There is little suggestion that any effort should be made to preserve them: recording was the main aim. As for many other counties, that for Norfolk was never completed and only the first two volumes, published in 1901 and 1906, have appeared. That such a project should have been undertaken is an indication of the growing interest in local history, but very much as part of the national story. 'It will trace, County by County, the story of England's growth from its prehistoric condition, through the barbarous age, the settlement of alien peoples and the gradual welding of many races into a nation that is now the greatest on the globe.'[50] In counties where the work was completed the majority of the text involved manorial histories arranged by hundred, very much as the early county histories had been. In Norfolk the work did not progress beyond the two introductory volumes, which covered in detail the geology and natural history of the county followed by general chapters covering prehistory to the medieval period. All known sites were marked on a map, showing that the main archeological sites in the county had been identified by this date. There followed chapters on political and ecclesiastical history (by Augustus Jessopp), religious houses, medieval painting and early Christian art. The chapter on religious houses reflected the current interest in documentary and legal history. The various charters granted to the religious houses are listed, but there is no attempt to describe the remains.

The clergy were also well represented in the Norfolk and Norwich Naturalists' Society. Loudon, writing in 1822, had recommended the study of 'natural history' as a suitable pastime for the clergy. He regarded it as

> superior, in a social point of view, even to a taste in gardening. The sportsman often follows his amusements to the great annoyance of his parishioners ... and the classical or indoor student of any kind secludes himself in his closet or laboratory, but the naturalist is abroad in the fields ... not only invigorating his health, but affording ample opportunity for frequent intercourse with his parishioners. In this way their reciprocal acquaintance is cultivated, and the clergyman at last becomes an advisor and friend as well as a spiritual teacher.[51]

In his founding address of 1869 the first chairman of the NNNS, the Reverend J. Crompton, stated the aims of the new society. The members (which included ladies) should be 'scientific but not destructive', and it should cover all branches of study. Some of its aims were surprisingly modern. It was to 'assist the rights of the poor and our own rights in keeping footpaths open', to 'bring entomological knowledge to bear on agriculture' and to 'set our faces against the perpetual gunning and destruction of birds'. This final aim must have run counter to the activities of some of the founding members, who, no doubt, were collectors of 'specimens'.[52] This early interest in footpaths reflects the needs and wide social membership of the Society, which was predominantly urban, at a time when the enclosure of land, particularly heaths, and changing farming methods were leading to the loss of public rights of way whose banks and hedgerows had proved such rich habitats both for plants and hedgerow birds. In spite of the improved transport links with Norwich's hinterlands, pleas were frequently made to 'our country friends' to attend meetings and contribute papers. Excursions were organised and meetings, at which papers by members were read, were well attended. 'We have stirred up a common interest in the beautiful works that are our study.'[53]

Many well-known and influential nineteenth-century Norfolk naturalists were members. Among them were Henry Stevenson (whose evidence helped to frame the Wild Birds Protection Acts passed from 1880 onwards) and author Arthur Patterson, the son of a Yarmouth shoemaker who also wrote for the local newspapers. He was the most prolific writer on the Broadland wildlife and his many books helped to popularise the natural history of the east coast and the Broads. His *Wild Fowlers and Poachers* (1929) described the precarious living made out of the thousands of wild fowl that congregated on Breydon Water, where payments for any rarities discovered and shot were a useful supplement to meagre earnings. As well as these men, other influential names included John Henry Gurney and the Lord Lieutenant of Norfolk, Russell Colman.

By the late nineteenth century the declining numbers of various species of birds and plants were becoming obvious. This was blamed on the destruction of heaths, the draining of marshes, the increasing activities of collectors and the number of visitors to what were becoming popular tourist areas, particularly along the coast and in the Broads. In his presidential address to the NNNA in

1892 Mr Wheeler drew attention to this by saying that one of the most permanently useful employments of the Society was to collect and record details of specimens becoming rare and extinct.[54]

## The early tourist industry

At the same time as the wealthy were enjoying their exclusive form of recreation within their walled parks and across the farmland of their tenants, a wider section of the population was also finding its way to Norfolk. It is no coincidence that the peak of game preservation in the late Victorian and Edwardian era should correspond with a rapid growth of interest in animal and plant life and rural amenities generally. Each was a function of the greater amount of leisure time and ease of travel. A more mobile middle-class group arrived, often by train, to the coastal resorts and the Norfolk Broads.

Visitors came as amateur botanists and photographers as well as sailors, golfers and simply to enjoy the seaside. It was these groups who were behind the founding of the early conservation societies. The National Footpaths Preservation Society was set up in 1884 and the National Trust in 1894. The inaugural meeting of the National Trust was held in the offices of the Commons Preservation Society, originally founded to safeguard the rapidly disappearing open spaces around London. Rambling clubs would meet at London stations for a day out walking in the country. For instance, in July 1891 The Vegetarian Rambling Club set out by train for Ely and from there to Stoke Ferry to visit, after an hour's walk, the fruit colony at Methwold in the Fens, where they were shown round by the colonists. 'The points which came up for discussion proved so engrossing, that little time was left to reach Stoke Ferry Station, so we had to step out, and the genial afternoon caused us to be in a delightful glow when we took our seats in the train.'[55]

As well as the coastal seaside resorts, the Norfolk Broads soon felt the brunt of this new tourist industry. An early promoter of the area through his writings was George Christopher Davies, who moved to Norfolk in 1889 and later became clerk to the County Council. He enjoyed the activities that the Broads provided, such as sailing, fishing, wild fowling and natural history. As well as writing a popular boys' adventure novel which Arthur Patterson claimed had inspired his interest in the area, he produced guide books. *Norfolk broads and rivers* and *A handbook to the broads and rivers of Norfolk and Suffolk*, both published in 1882, went into many editions.[56] Books on the area proliferated and the joys of 'gipsy-ing in East Anglian Waters' were extolled.[57] The shooting of wild fowl, the study-ing of plants and animals, sailing and the pursuit of the novel hobby of photography were all enjoyed by these early visitors. The flowers along the banks made a 'changing panorama of kaleidoscopic beauty', while the windmills and the wherries gliding past with their distinctive large brown sails were painted, photographed and commented upon. It was not only the quiet and sup-posedly unchanging landscape of the Broads that attracted interest, but the inhabitants, who were also seen as possessing the self-sufficient and independ-ent personalities which were coming to be attributed to the countryman. In 1905 W.A. Dutt described the eel catchers, 'almost the sole survivors of the passing race of real Broadsmen ... who lived in isolated cottages on lonesome marsh-lands and spent days and nights on the rivers and fens were of a freedom-loving and self-reliant type'.[58] All these urban middle-class commentators and visitors were in search of an archaic, stable 'natural' world in a period when, increas-ingly, economic collapse and political turbulence were the realities from which they wished to escape. The areas of marsh and water may have been unproduc-tive in agricultural terms, but 'They are silent with a vast agricultural and indus-trial silence, they speak to the man who has leisure, temporary or permanent, for the study of Nature and the little subjects of her kingdom.'[59]

Those with an archaeological interest were also travelling. Before the days of the railway, enthusiasm for archaeology and historic sites was confined to the elite and it was only men such as Dawson Turner who could set out to visit, paint and describe the locations featured in Blomefield's book. By the middle of the nineteenth century, and particularly with the arrival of the railway, middle-class tourism in search of the historical was increasing, partly as a result of the patri-otism which grew during the Napoleonic Wars and continued with the estab-lishment of the empire, and partly encouraged by the vogue for historical novels which began with the works of Sir Walter Scott. A casual, but no doubt typical, traveller was the vicar of Dereham, who, in 1869, described the pleasures of 'vagabonding': 'You take your wife and child, a telescope and a county map in

*14 The atmosphere which tourists were seeking is clearly illustrated in this picture of the eel catcher in his boat on Rockland Broad in* Norfolk Broads and Rivers, *by G.C. Davies (1884).*

your phaeton — start when you please, go where you please and return when you please.'[60] The railway and bicycle opened up opportunities for far more people to visit sites and buildings, and the pages of the nineteenth-century volumes of *Norfolk Archaeology* feature rood screens, wall paintings, pulpits and fonts, reflecting the interests of many of the members.

Reports of the excursions organised by the NNAS first appear in *Norfolk Archaeology* in 1910, when members of the society met at Eccles Road station and then went by carriages to Wilby Old Hall and church, the remains of Kenninghall Palace, South Lopham hand-loom manufactory and church and Blo Norton, Garboldisham and East Harling churches before returning to Norwich from Harling Road station. However, it was the arrival of the motor car which really allowed visits to the countryside to increase to an unprecedented level. 'The introduction of motor cars for those who take part in excursions marks the beginning of a new era',[61] wrote the excursion secretary of the Archaeology Society in 1911. He described how on the 1st September the society visited Holkham via Cawston, East Barsham, the pilgrim chapel at Houghton-on-the-hill and Houghton church. 'Owing to the distances to be covered, and the difficulty of finding enough carriages, recourse was made to motor cars, supplied by Messrs Howes and Sons, and gave general satisfaction.' After this very full day 'the party returned to Norwich in the beautiful sunset light'.[62] J.E. Vincent claimed his book, *Through East Anglia in a motor car,* published in 1907, to be the first designed for the motorist. Travelling with a driver and mechanic, he set out in 1906 from Cambridge to criss-cross the area. While his description covers the great houses, medieval castles and abbeys, he was unimpressed by the landscape. Of the salt marshes of the north coast he wrote, 'one feels no desire to see it again unless indeed it is, as by its appearance it may well be, a haunt of wildfowl worth shooting'.[63]

By the early twentieth century, therefore, we find that interest in the wildlife and antiquities of Norfolk had moved beyond the narrow confines of the serious academic. Increased leisure, the ability to travel and the availability of popular literature, alongside the very obvious expansion of towns and the destruction of habitats and historic buildings (sometimes through over-restoration), meant that a national concern for legislation to provide protection was gathering pace.

1   For a biography of Sir Thomas Browne see R. Barbour (2013) *Sir Thomas Browne: A Life*. Oxford, Oxford University Press.
2   E. Fowler (1976) 'Some Norfolk naturalists', in Norfolk Naturalists Trust (ed.), *Nature in Norfolk: a heritage in trust*. Norwich, Jarrold and Sons, 9.
3   For details of Robert Marsham's life and tree planting see R.W. Ketton-Cremer (1948) *A Norfolk gallery*. London, Faber, 149-61.
4   NRO MC 60A, transcript of *Indications of Spring 1738-1788*.
5   R.W. Ketton-Cremer (1944) *Norfolk Portraits*. London, Faber, 96-109.
6   A. Dain (2004) 'An enlightened and polite society', in C. Rawcliffe and R. Wilson (eds), Norwich since 1550. London and New York, Hambledon and London, 197.
7   Dain 2004, 202.
8   J.E. Smith (1804) *Trans Linnean Society of London* 7, 295-301. << AQ: not in biblio - please provide all details inc title >>
9   Quoted in A. Bull (1999) 'The Norfolk botanists', in G. Beckett and A. Bull, *A Flora of Norfolk*. Kings Lynn, G. Becket, 36.
10  H.D. Geldart (1913) 'Presidential address', TNNNS 9, 643-90, passim.
11  N. Goodman, (ed.) (2007) *Dawson Turner: a Norfolk antiquary and his remarkable family*. Chichester, Phillimore, passim.
12  Bull 1999, 40.

13  White, W. (1883) *History, Gazetteer, and Directory of Norfolk*. London: Simpkin, Marshall, & Co., 107.

14  Quoted in D.E. Allen (1976) *The naturalist in Britain: a social history*. London, Allen Lane, 143.

15  White 1883, 106.

16  H. Stevenson (1872) 'Presidential address', *TNNNT* 1:3, 7-19, 14.

17  M. Ewans (1992) *The battle for the Broads*. Lavenham, Terence Dalton, 48.

18  White 1883, 105.

19  Holkham MS H/bnB1

20  Holkham MS F/4E/M2/38

21  S. Wade Martins and T. Williamson (2008) *The countryside of East Anglia: changing landscapes 1870-1950*. Woodbridge, Boydell and Brewer, 92.

22  White 1883, 105.

23  Allen 1976, 143.

24  B. Green, MS notes.

25  F. Johnson (1929) 'John Kirkpatrick, antiquary', *Norfolk Archaeology* 23, 285-304

26  H. Ninham (1864) *Views of the ancient city gates of Norwich as they appeared in 1722*. Norwich, Cundill, Miller and Leavins, ii.

27  J. Walpole (1997) *Art and artists of the Norwich School*. Woodbridge, Antique Collectors' Club, passim.

28  B. Green, MS notes.

29  R.W. Ketton Cremer (1952) 'The rector of Fersfield', *Norfolk Archaeology* 30, 365-9.

30  Title page of F. Blomefield, *An essay towards a topographical history of Norfolk* (1805 edition).

31  G.A. Stephen (1921) 'Francis Blomefield's queries in preparation for his History of Norfolk', *Norfolk Archaeology* 20, 1-10.

32  M.F. Serpell (1983) 'Sir John Fenn, his friends and the Paston Letters', *Antiquaries Journal* 63:1, 95-121.

33  E. Impey (2008) *Castle Acre Priory and Castle*. Swindon, English Heritage, 46.

34  BL MSS Add. 23013-23066, 29738.

35  D. McKitterick (2007) 'Dawson Turner and his book collecting', in N. Goodman (ed.) *Dawson Turner: a Norfolk antiquary and his remarkable family*. Chichester, Phillimore, 88.

36  Quoted in Allen 1976, 158

37  MS Museum accession books vol 1. Norwich Castle Museum

38  J. Rodziewicz (2013) 'Making a museum out of a Norman keep and Victorian prison: The Norfolk and Norwich Museum 1886-1896', *Norfolk Archaeology* 46, 503-10.

39  A. Woodson-Boulton (2008) 'Victorian Museums and Victorian society', *History Compass* 6, 109-46; C. Yanni (2005) *Nature's museums: Victorian science and the architecture of display*. New York, Princeton University Press, passim.

40  S. Piggott (1976) *Ruins in a landscape*. Edinburgh, Edinburgh University Press, 181.

41  Piggott 1976, 175.

42  B. Cozens-Hardy (1946) 'The early days of the Society', *Norfolk Archaeology* 29, 1-7.

43  A.J. Lawson (1981) 'The Barrows of Norfolk', in A.J. Lawson, E.A. Martin and D. Priddy, *The Barrows of East Anglia*. *East Anglian Archaeology* 12, Gressenhall, Norfolk Museums Service, 37-8.

44  A.D. Saunders (1983) 'A century of ancient monument legislation, 1882-1983', *Antiquaries Journal* 63, 18.

45  A. Jessopp (1894) *The Trials of a Country Parson*. London, Fisher-Unwin, 143.

46  A. Pevsner and B. Wilson (1997) *Buildings of England, Norfolk*, 2 vols. London, Penguin, 257.

47  I am grateful to Michael Begley for this information.

48  *Victoria County History, Norfolk* 1, 1901, vii.

49  *Victoria County History, Norfolk* 1, 1901, ix.

50  *Victoria County History, Norfolk* 1, 1901, vii.

51  J.C. Loudon (1822) *Magazine of Natural History*, quoted in Allen 1976, 22.

52  *TNNNS* 1, 1869-74, 18.

53  *TNNNS* 1, 1869-74, 18.

54  *TNNNS* 5, 1892, 235-49.

55  *The Independent Vegetarian Advocate* 11 July 1891, 43.

56  Ewans 1992, 69-70.

57  H.M. Doughty (1897) *Summer in Broadland*. London, Jarrolds, frontispiece.

58  W.A. Dutt (1905) *The Norfolk Broads*. London, Methuen, 83.

59  J. Bygott (1923) *Eastern England*. London, Routledge, 151.

60  *Armstrong's Norfolk Diary* 1963, 32.

61  *Norfolk Archaeology* 18, 1914, i.

62  *Norfolk Archaeology* 18, 1914, xvi-xx.

63  J.E. Vincent (1907) *Norfolk Archaeology*. London, Methuen, 336.

# 2

# The state steps in: the beginnings of national legislation

Early legislation to protect birds, mammals and fishes was more concerned with sustaining an economic resource than the conservation of rare or endangered species. By the end of the sixteenth century there were acts intended to prevent over-fishing and the killing of wildfowl during the breeding season in the Broads. However, it is unlikely that they were ever enforced. A further act of 1770 made it illegal to net, drive or take teal, wigeon and other waterfowl between July and August because of 'the great damage and decay of the breed of wildfowl'. Again, this act, along with those protecting the fisheries, was widely flouted. In 1857 the Norwich and Norfolk Anglers' Society was founded to protect fish stocks which were suffering from poaching and over-fishing.[1]

This all changed in the second half of the nineteenth century, which saw a growing concern over the destruction of both ancient monuments and wildlife and the beginnings of efforts to legislate to protect both. This was stimulated by an increasing awareness of the gradual spread of towns and cities alongside industrialisation, and the growing ease of transport for a greater proportion of a rising population. Spurred on by education and a growing middle class, an awareness of natural and cultural history, stimulated also by the popularity of romantic poets, novelists and artists, was becoming common among more than just the traditional landowners. National societies for the protection of the countryside were proliferating, the earliest of which was the Commons Preservation Society (1869). While many, such as the Smoke Abatement Society, had very specific aims others, such as the National Trust and the Selborne Society, named after the famous naturalist Gilbert White of Selborne and founded in 1885, were more general. In fact, in an address to the Selborne Society in 1900 Mr Bryce stated that societies aimed at the preservation of nature should be linked to those caring for ancient monuments.[2] However, legislation for the protection of the natural and historical elements of the environment remained strictly separated.

## Protecting the natural world

A worry for the Norfolk naturalist Henry Stevenson was the decline in the numbers of birds and plants. In his 1871 presidential address to the NNNS he said that 'the preservation of indigenous species should be a primary object of all natural history societies' and that 'the wholesale system of egging, carried out in this county in years gone by, has done almost as much as gunners and enterprising agriculturalists put together to banish certain species from their former haunts'. He went on to give several examples of the decline in bird numbers, including a colony of lesser terns at Salthouse which was 'all but exterminated' by a gunner who also took the eggs. 'I look to an influence arising out of the proceedings of such societies as this, to create an interest in the preservation of all indigenous species.'[3] Stevenson himself became a prominent campaigner for the first act of parliament to protect birds.

This early concern with birdlife was to be found in other parts of the country, particularly along the Northumberland coast, where sea birds and their eggs were being taken in ever-increasing numbers. This lead to the Sea Birds Protection Act of 1869, which provided for a closed season from the first of April to the first of August to protect thirty-three named species of sea birds. A further act of 1876 extended the closed season and the number of birds covered. The fact that the new laws were regularly flouted led to the formation of the Breydon Wild Birds Protection Society in 1888 (one of the earliest in the country) under the chairmanship of Henry Buxton, followed shortly by the Cley and Blakeney Bird

WATCHER'S HUT ON BREYDON WATER

SHORE SHOOTING ON BREYDON

15  *The watcher on Breydon Water employed by the Breydon Wild Birds Protection Society (above).
Below: a shooter with his dog, as illustrated in A.H. Patterson,* Nature in Eastern Norfolk *(1905)*

Preservation Trust in 1901 and similar bodies at Wells and Wolferton, each with their own watcher during the breeding season.[4] Gradually a greater respect for wildlife was developing, particularly at Breydon Water, under the able and eagle eyes of the watchers, the first of whom was 'Ducky' Chambers, who kept meticulous notes of what he saw. In 1921 W.G. Clarke wrote in support of the Protection Society, pointing out that 'It is doubtful that any other area of like size in the British Isles has been visited by so many rare birds.'[5]

A further act of 1894 enabled county councils to introduce protection for certain species and also covered the protection of eggs as well as the birds themselves. County councils were also encouraged to identify areas for protection, and Norfolk County Council set up its own Wild Birds Protection Committee which singled out the Norfolk Broads and much of the north Norfolk coast for protection. An order was issued in 1895 making it an offence to take or destroy the eggs of any wild bird on Hickling Broad, Horsey Mere, Marham Broad and adjoining fens and marshes, as well as the Broads of Ormesby, Rollesby and Filby. Concern was expressed about the declining numbers of avocets, black terns, blue tailed godwits, ruffs, bearded tits, great crested grebe, gagany and summer teal – all of which were suffering from shooting and persistent egging. Parts of the north coast around Wells were already protected, the earl of Leicester providing watchers, but much of the coastal marshes from Stiffkey to Wolferton now became a protected area. Here it was terns, dotterels, redshank, oystercatchers and shelduck which were seen as the most endangered. Now for the first time areas were identified as reserves, rather than just the birds – a policy which received enthusiastic support from the NNNS.[6] However, all these laws were impossible to enforce. Local police could not monitor the remote areas of marsh and fen and the identification of these sites as special areas simply drew them to the attention of collectors.

The Society for the Protection of Birds was founded in Manchester in 1889 and received a royal charter in 1904. Its primary function was stopping the slaughter of wild birds for plumage and in its early years its resources were concentrated on promoting plumage bills. These efforts were finally successful in 1926. However, its interest had rapidly widened, with the employing of watchers to protect rare species, and it was influential in lobbying for further acts in 1896, 1902 and 1904 that gave protection to more birds and extended the closed season. However, very few cases were brought and any fines were far outweighed by the potential profits from selling eggs and specimens.

As we have seen, the members of the local societies were mainly urban dwellers and from the trading and professional classes as well as some more eminent citizens and authors. The exceptions to this urban bias were the rural clergymen and members of the gentry. In the main, however, it was an urban membership, who could easily make the meetings where their voices could be heard. As the population of Norwich expanded in the second half of the nineteenth century the countryside became increasingly remote from the city dwellers, who thus enjoyed the novelty of an outing to the countryside, with its hedgerows and footpaths. These were the people who were likely to press for the protection of valuable habitats – something that was in fact supported by many of the leading landlords, some of whom were county councillors and members of the Wild Birds Protection Committee and were happy to see egg and specimen collectors excluded from their land during closed seasons.

## Protecting historic monuments

While bird protection was receiving attention from the natural historians, efforts to protect the cultural landscape were rather slower to get off the ground. As early as 1788 Richard Gough, in a letter to the *Gentleman's Magazine*, had called for the valuing of some buildings as 'national objects' which should be subjected to 'proper study' and whose preservation should be deliberate rather than 'left to mere chance'. He suggested that the Society of Antiquaries should take an active role. Correspondence on the subject continued[7] and in 1841 John Britton, in evidence to a House of Commons Committee, suggested that monuments such as historic houses and Roman villas deserved protection.[8] By the 1820s the government was recognising the growing interest in the monuments of the past and in 1828 the Tower of London was first opened to the public by the Board of Ordnance. This move, feeding on the growing nationalism of the century, was an immediate success. However, any attempts to interfere with the rights of landowners over archaeological sites and monuments on their lands were bound to run into trouble.

The work of the Society for the Protection of Ancient Buildings (SPAB) (founded 1877) drew attention to the dangers of the over-restoration of churches and other medieval buildings and alerted public opinion to the destruction and loss of the country's national heritage. This concern was not always reflected in the national and local antiquarian societies, whose interest tended to be focused on excavations aimed at the collection of artefacts, which, in the process, destroyed sites. Early reports of the proceedings of the committee meetings of the NNAS consist very much of 'exhibiting finds'. In 1859, for instance, these included a silver badge and pin, an umpalla, several medieval coins and a 'seventeenth century ink bottle'.[9]

One of the most eminent of the early excavators was General Pitt Rivers, who owned some of the richest archaeological areas in England in what is now a UNESCO World Heritage Site on Cannock Chase in Wiltshire. Concern over the loss of sites was brought to the fore with the destruction of parts of the stone circle at Avebury (in Wiltshire) by the removal of stones and the building of new cottages within the stone circle. The cause of preservation was taken up by the avid collector and student of Charles Darwin, John Lubbock (later Lord Avebury). With a family fortune made through banking he was able to follow his scientific interests, which took him from natural history to archaeology and prehistory. Although a collector, he was aware that the aim of collection should be the study of the objects and the light they shed on past cultures rather than collection for its own sake. He was also concerned for the future of the monuments of the period and was much influenced by the system of state protection that already existed in Denmark. As MP for Maidstone he made several attempts in the 1870s to introduce legislation to protect ancient monuments but opposition was fierce, as landowners resented what they saw as unwarranted interference in private affairs.[10] In the heated debate that took place in the Commons, the Tory MP Francis Hervey voiced a typical concern when he asked 'are the absurd relics of our barbarian predecessors, who found time hanging heavily on their hands, and set about piling up great barrows and rings of stones, to be preserved at the cost of infringement to property rights?'[11] Lubbock's bill did, however, gain a degree of mild support from the press. The *Times* remarked that 'it would be a great thing to have it ... recognized by law that national monuments are really monuments of national concern'.[12] The bill failed to pass, but Lubbock continued to fight for it and his concern was so great that he bought Silbury Hill, West Kennett long barrow and Hackpen Hill to protect them.

By 1882 even Lubbock realised that statutory protection would not be accepted and instead suggested an ancient monuments inspectorate that could bring to owners' attention the importance of monuments in their care and persuade them to hand them over to state control. The result was the Ancient Monuments Act of 1882, which, as only a permissive act with no teeth, had very limited powers. There was no provision for compulsory acquisition by the state; instead, owners could voluntarily put sites in state care – a practice known as 'guardianship'. Lord Carnarvon (of Tutankhamun fame), in his anniversary address to the Society of Antiquaries, described the act as being in 'a mutilated condition, shorn of its many original provisions, crippled in its powers and limited in its scope'.[13] However, it did establish the concept of a 'schedule' of monuments which owners could then make over into the State's guardianship while reserving the freehold to themselves. It also established an Inspectorate of Ancient Monuments, with General Pitt Rivers as its first Inspector. Much of the groundwork had already been done, with a list of target sites published by Kains-Jackson in 1880.[14]

It was central to Pitt Rivers' and Lubbock's strategy that ancient monuments should be accurately surveyed and Pitt Rivers travelled tirelessly across much of Britain, recording with the help of drawings, watercolours and photographs sites to be included in the schedule of sites he would like to see protected. He had been surveying archaeological sites for twenty years and so was well qualified for the task. He travelled by train first class, with his assistants in third class. Hired carriages carried them between railway stations, hotels and the monuments. Central southern England was comprehensively covered, as were the Midlands, Wales, north-west England and Scotland, including the Orkneys. Eastern England was the largest area left unvisited and the south-east warranted only a single visit.[15] His notebooks are now in the Pitt Rivers Museum in Oxford. Progress was slow, with owners reluctant to relinquish control of their property, and only twenty-two sites across England and Wales were in guardianship by the late 1880s, all of them prehistoric and uninhabited. Stone circles and tumuli predominated. Lubbock explained this preference in his preface to Kains-Jackson's book. Medieval remains should be dealt with in a different manner because they would be more expensive to maintain and there would always be controversy as to how far any 'restoration' should go.

An Office of Works with specialist staff was established with the aim of maintaining monuments. They were to 'avoid, as far as possible, anything which can be considered in the nature of restoration, to do nothing that would impair the archaeological interest of the monuments and to confine themselves rigorously to such works as may be necessary to ensure their stability, to accentuate their interest and to perpetuate their existence in the form in which they have come down to us'.[16] However, Pitt Rivers became despondent as he saw important sites destroyed with no power to prevent it; in 1890 he resigned his salary, although he continued as Inspector in a voluntary capacity. The act was doomed to have little impact, with neither political will nor public support to make it a success.[17] It was amended in 1889 to include medieval sites, whereby any structure of 'historic or architectural interest' could be added to the schedule, but fines for destruction were always small and provided little in the way of a deterrent. In 1891 Pitt Rivers wrote to Lubbock that little reliance could be placed on government. He even questioned whether 'it is right to tax the people for the maintenance of Antiquities, which none but the educated classes, and not all of them, are in a position to appreciate'. Instead, owners and local archaeological societies should be encouraged to do the work. 'No inspector of Ancient Monuments can stand sentry over all the Monuments in Great Britain'.[18]

While Lubbock's bill was bogged down in the House of Commons, the most obvious case for the need to protect historic buildings could be seen immediately outside on the Victoria Embankment. This was a period when improvements in roads and the development of railways were leading to considerable destruction of the historic fabric of the capital. Protests from SPAB led in 1879 to the retention of Balthasar Gerbier's Water Gate in a hollow in the Embankment. In 1889 the London County Council was created with John Lubbock as a prominent member and chairman from 1890 to 1892. Under his influence the Council was given powers by Parliament to purchase buildings or places of historic interest. There followed in 1894 the beginning of a detailed survey of London which was completed in 1896. This pioneering work was to prove a model for later survey work, including that of the Royal Commissions set up in 1908 (see below).[19]

An important step was taken in 1900, when the scope of national legislation was widened to include 'any structure of historic or architectural interest or any remains thereof'. Inhabited buildings were not included, as such a measure would never have been passed by a parliament jealous of property rights and concerned about interference with an individual's home.[20] County councils were given the powers both to prosecute those who damaged protected sites and to maintain sites and open them to the public, and several towns took advantage of this to take control of their city walls. This power was strengthened in 1909, when local authorities were encouraged to preserve 'objects of historic interest or natural beauty'.

However, the British system of protecting monuments was still far behind that in many European countries and the 1900s saw further demands for improved legislation. This was highlighted in a book published in 1905 by the professor of Fine Art at Edinburgh University, Baldwin Brown, entitled *The Care of Ancient Monuments*. In this he recommended the setting up of an agency to create an inventory of 'the artistic and historical treasures we possess'. This he saw as a necessary step before any such heritage could be protected. An attempt was made through the Congress of Archaeological Societies, set up in 1888, to coordinate research and survey.[21] A conference of delegates attended by twenty-four local societies, including that for Norfolk, was held at Burlington House in London in July 1889 and local societies were encouraged 'to procure six-inch scale maps and on them record the localities of all finds, field names and so on and to be on the watch for the destruction of antiquities, so as to bring public opinion to bear upon the destroyers.'[22] Very little was achieved nationally and there is no further mention of the idea in the pages of *Norfolk Archaeology*. Instead a state initiative was needed, and in 1908 the Board of Works set up the Royal Commission on Ancient and Historical Monuments in England (RCAHME), with similar commissions in Wales and Scotland. The first county to be surveyed was Hertfordshire and this was followed by others, but the work was detailed and slow and only a fifth of the country was covered in the Commission's first fifty years. Norfolk was not one of these, but those volumes that were completed demonstrated the wealth of sites that existed and strengthened the case for their preservation.[23]

The development of national legislation can often be linked to key episodes in which decisive steps had to be taken in response to individual crises which aroused the public's awareness of a threat to cherished buildings and sites. Such a change in attitude can be dated to the return of Lord Curzon to Britain from India, where he had instigated a survey of archaeology. Back in his homeland he was horrified to hear of the proposed sale of Tattershall Castle (Lincolnshire) in 1911 to an American who had already removed the fine medieval fireplaces for shipment to the United States. They had been removed before Lord Curzon was able to buy the castle, but he managed to recover them and restore them to their proper places. The episode aroused much public interest and pressure for legislation. The result was the Monuments Consolidation and Amendment Act of 1913, which finally began a national programme of scheduling monuments and bringing the most important into the guardianship of the state. The Government acknowledged for the first time that the state had a cultural responsibility for the physical remains of its own history. The Commissioner of Works was empowered to set up an advisory body (the Ancient Monuments Board) to help in its work. They were expected to apply the qualification of 'national importance' to monuments being considered for guardianship: their actual and relative importance and their topographical value. It was the duty of commissioners to prepare a list of monuments whose preservation seemed to the Ancient Monuments Board to be of national importance. These were listed in various categories: monastic and military buildings; town walls; crosses; bridges; Roman remains; and earthworks. Bridges were seen as particularly at risk, as a Ministry of Transport Act had set aside £10,000,000 for bridge improvements. Important weaknesses in the act were that it did not cover inhabited or ecclesiastical buildings in use. The owner of a scheduled monument had to notify the Commission of any proposed works and a 'Preservation Order' could be placed on any monument seen as in danger. An 'ancient monument' was defined as 'a structure or erection not inhabited or in ecclesiastical use, the preservation of which was in the public interest by virtue of its special historical, architectural, traditional, artistic or archaeological interest – or the site of any such monument or its remains'. Local authorities could become owners and could assist in the cost of maintenance, whether they owned the monument or not.[24] In Norfolk some of the most impressive castle ruins, such as the fifteenth-century brick-built Caister Castle (made famous by its connection with Sir John Falstaff) and the twelfth-century keep and massive earthworks at Castle Rising Castle, along with the two

16 *The twelfth-century castle at Castle Rising, with its substantial earthworks, was one of the first sites to be scheduled under the 1913 Ancient Monuments Act.*

abbeys at Walsingham and St Benet's, were scheduled in 1915, as were medieval buildings in Norwich, including the castle. After this first burst of activity, most scheduling had to wait until the 1920s and no sites were brought into state guardianship to be opened to the public until then.

While the state was slowly gaining powers to protect monuments, research into Norfolk's archaeology continued, but often in a destructive way. While some of the objects recovered were finding their way to Norwich Museum, much still went unrecorded. At least forty-six barrow excavations took place between 1900 and 1950, of which very few records remain. An important figure in encouraging the proper recording of the activities of prehistoric man was W.G. Clarke (1877-1925), author of *In Breckland wilds*. In 1908 he initiated a meeting of local prehistorians in rooms of the Norfolk and Norwich Library to inaugurate 'an East Anglian Society for the study of all matters pertaining to prehistoric man'. Their

concern was the recording, mapping, publication and preservation of monuments and they fed on the great enthusiasm of the time for collecting flint implements from the light soils of Breckland. The society soon expanded and in 1935
became the national Prehistoric Society, which has since developed an international reputation for prehistoric studies.[25]

## The beginnings of the conservation movement

As more people came to know the countryside, even if it was only as weekend
cyclists or through a fortnight's visit in the summer, they somehow felt they had
a stake in its future, and there was a huge increase in interest in rural affairs.
'The symbolic importance of the countryside grew as its economic and social
importance was eclipsed.'[26] The fiercest struggles over its future were not
between town and country (country people remained idealised but neglected –
– a point fiercely made by A.G. Street in his article 'A countryman's view')[27] but
rather between classes, as reflected in differing recreational tastes.

At the top end of the social scale, *Country Life* had begun publication in 1897
and was an immediate success, particularly among town dwellers. Articles,
accompanied by fine photography, covered both wildlife and historic buildings,
especially churches and great houses. It was partly responsible for popularising
interest in architectural history and particularly the country house. On a lower
rung of the socially ladder were the 'trippers' who left litter, picked flowers and
required 'tea shacks' lining the main roads for refreshment.

It is against this background of increasing interest in and appreciation of the
countryside as a place for recreation, where some areas were simply too important because of their zoology, botany or archaeology to be left to property developers or food producers, that the beginnings of the conservation movement in
the county can be seen. While many of its advocates were to be found not among
the native country dwellers but among those who came with fresh eyes into
rural areas, some established local landowners, such as the Buxton and Gurney
families, were prominent in their calls for the protection of the countryside. John
Buxton realised the importance for wildlife of Horsey Mere, which he gave to
the National Trust, while Robert and Eustace Gurney recognised that any calls

for special protection for some areas must be backed by scientific evidence. For this reason in 1901 they set up the first-ever freshwater laboratory beside the heavily silted-up Sutton Broad. They built a house with accommodation for four or five workers and an attached laboratory at a remote location at Longmoor Point. Here they employed scientists to work on the flora and fauna of the broad. They also planned to encourage the study of the relationship of animals to their environment as well as tidal influences on marine biology. A scheme drawn up with the NNNS for a botanical study of the Norfolk Broads was planned for 1908.[28] This work fed into many papers by Robert Gurney published in the Transactions of the NNNS, and particularly his presidential address of 1913, 'The origins and conditions of the existence of the fauna of freshwaters'.

## The National Trust

Concerns about the destruction of wildlife in Norfolk and East Anglia were part of a national realisation. One of the aims of the National Trust, formed in 1894 and incorporated by parliament in 1907, was 'the preservation (so far as practicable) of the natural aspect, features and animal and plant life', and it was the earliest body to be actively involved in the ownership of sites in the region. While nineteenth-century Norfolk naturalists were concentrating their activity in the Broads, Brecks and along the coast, large tracts of diverse natural habitats were being lost to agriculture in the west of the county. The draining of the fens has been described as 'our greatest ecological disaster'.[29] Only at Wicken Fen, across the border in Cambridgeshire, had the value of sedge led to the survival of a small piece of sedge fen and, by the mid-nineteenth century, its importance as one of the last places where the fen orchid could be found and the diversity of its insect life were recognised by local naturalists. Insect collecting became a small local industry; so much so that there was a danger of over-collection of the distinctive insects and plants surviving on this last undrained relic of the Cambridgeshire fenland.[30] The decline in the demand for sedge, alongside rumours that the the fen might be drained, prompted entomologists to begin buying portions of the site. J.C. Moberley bought two acres in 1893, which he then sold to the National Trust, and in 1899 Charles Rothschild bought thirty

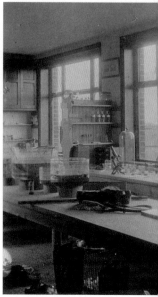

17 *In 1901 Robert and Eustace Gurney built the first ever freshwater marine laboratory in a remote position on Sutton Broad, where pioneer research was undertaken until the outbreak of the First World War. Top: the Sutton Laboratory exterior; left and above: the laboratory interior.*

acres, which he donated to the Trust, and so the foundations of the first National Trust Nature Reserve had been laid. The dipterist G.H. Verrall was also buying piecemeal, so that, by the time of his death in 1910, he owned 220 acres, which was added to the National Trust's holding.[31]

Charles Rothschild, with a banking fortune behind him, was a great supporter of the aims of the National Trust and by 1912 he was a member of its Council, serving on the Wicken Fen Management Committee. While being involved in the affairs of the family bank, his main interest was in natural history. This enthusiasm had been kindled by his brother Walter, who was ten years his senior. Walter was responsible for the collection of a vast museum of natural history

*Laboratory staff in 1909.*

Ǥ.A.Potts.    Fryer.    H.M.Fuchs
Sept. 1909.

at the family home in Tring, which eventually found its way to the British Museum. Charles' main interest was in butterflies and moths and, before he left school, he had co-authored a two-volume book on the subject. After school at Harrow, upon which he looked back with horror, Charles went to Cambridge to read natural science and then set out on the first of many world-wide trips collecting specimens. By 1907 he was a world authority on fleas.[32]

A second site that owed its acquisition by the National Trust largely to the generosity of Charles Rothschild was the great shingle spit of Blakeney Point in north Norfolk, which was donated to the Trust in 1912. For several years Francis Wall Oliver (1864–1951), professor of botany at University College London, had been taking students to the Broads to introduce them to the new subject of ecology. In 1908 he visited the Point and realised its potential for study. In 1910 he persuaded the university to purchase the old lifeboat house from the RNLI to be used for field courses. With his students, he investigated the ornithology, botany, entomology and growth of salt marshes behind the advancing shingle spits at the Point. He leased the Point from Lord Calthorpe and gained permission to build a field laboratory on the spit as a base for his research. A brick field laboratory and dark room were built in 1913 next to the corrugated iron former lifeboat house with the help of a grant from the Sladen Trustees, who administered funds for the promotion of research in natural history. It contained benches for microscopes as well as for chemical and physical work on the bacteriology of soils. There were also balance and dark rooms. (Until 1986 accommodation for students was in tents, but in that year the laboratory was moved to the old lifeboat house and the brick building converted to accommodation).

Blakeney Point was included in A.G. Tansley's four-week field excursion of 1911, organised for an international group of phytogeographical experts for which he edited and produced a guide book entitled *Types of British Vegetation*. In it he recognised the Point's importance, describing it as one of 'the best examples of wild Nature absolutely free from human interference'.[33] It was essential that such sites should be preserved for long-term survey and experimental work. When Lord Calthorpe died Professor Oliver took the initiative, negotiating its purchase from his executors and setting about raising the money. Fearing for its future, he led a public appeal for its purchase.

The National Trust took some persuading before Oliver convinced them of the wisdom of taking on Blakeney Point, but in 1912 the necessary £695 was raised, with considerable support from Lord Rothschild, and the site was handed over to the National Trust to be managed by the NNNS, thus forming the National Trust's first coastal nature reserve and setting a trend which was to continue after the First World War. With care and patience, the now-famous ternery was re-established.

Since 1912 the National Trust holding has been extended. In 1922 the lifeboat house (adjacent to the old lifeboat house) was acquired to provide a base for the watcher.[34] This mainly blue-painted corrugated iron structure is still a distinctive building on the skyline. The nearby Morston and Stiffkey marshes were acquired in the 1970s.

The National Trust was always short of money and negotiations over acquisition could be long and protracted. The charity's annual income did not keep pace with its acquisition of new properties, most of which needed expensive repairs and maintenance. Rothchild felt that nature reserves were being neglected and his support turned to disenchantment.[35] He was concerned that sites were acquired by the Trust as and when they became available rather than as the result of any rational plan. Worried by this rather random arrangement,

*18 The shingle spit of Blakeney Point was the first coastal reserve to be purchased by the National Trust, in 1912.*

which had little regard for national significance, Rothschild set about the establishment of a national society to take forward the case for nature reserves. The first formal meeting of the new Society for the Promotion of Nature Reserves (SPNR) took place at the British Museum (Natural History) in July 1912, with the main aims of undertaking a survey across the UK to produce a list of sites which should be secured and, where possible, obtaining them and then handing them over to the National Trust. At its founding meeting the Society stated its objectives, the first of which was to 'collect and collate information as to areas of land in the United Kingdom which retain primitive conditions and contain rare and local species liable to extinction owing to building, drainage, disafforestation, or in consequence of the cupidity of collectors'. The membership was never intended to be democratic, but its council, which was limited to fifty members, consisted of eminent biologists such as A.G. Tansley and influential figures in the social and political world. They would prepare schemes for site protection and if possible obtain sites for the National Trust. Their list was published in 1915 and included sites such as Blakeney Point and the Broads, described, along with seven others within the UK, as of 'primary importance', with Upton, Hickling, Barton and Horning Broads in Norfolk given grade one status.[36]

Although Blakeney Point was formally handed over to the National Trust shortly before SPNR's initial July meeting, it would seem to fit perfectly into the type of site to be considered in danger under their definition. This pristine four-mile spit of shingle backed by sand dunes and salt marshes provided a variety of habitats. It was particularly vulnerable to the activities of egg collectors who, on one Sunday each spring, 'Point Sunday', would board small boats towed by a larger one and go out to the Point to collect eggs.

Professor Oliver continued to bring students and carry out research which was published in a wide variety of academic journals. In 1913 he wrote that 'The recent acquisition of Blakeney Point by the National Trust as a nature reserve is, we may hope, a sign of the times. A wonderful collection of natural habitats has been secured by the wise generosity of donors against the possibility of any interference.'[37] According to one of Professor Oliver's distinguished students, Edward J. Salisbury, it was the type of multi-disciplinary survey developed by Oliver at Blakeney, looking at the physiography and vegetation of shingles, sand-hills and salt marsh as well as at the flora and fauna, that 'saved British ecology from becoming dominated by the more static description of vegetation units'.[38] It can thus be claimed that, through the work of Professor Oliver, Blakeney Point was the birthplace of ecology in the UK.

Oliver wrote a paper in May 1912 giving his views on how the reserve should be managed by the National Trust. Much of his advice would still be relevant today. He realised that the site needed to be maintained in its wild maritime state, while at the same time allowing naturalists to carry out research and visitors to enjoy (partial) access. To this end it would be important to gain local sympathy and understanding, and so the management committee should include a local element as well as a naturalist voice alongside the National Trust. Among the locals should be the former agent to Lord Calthorpe, who 'has much local influence and in consultation has been of much assistance in connection with the acquisition of the Point'. Shooting should be forbidden, but 'Norfolk is a land of field sports and this part of our programme will not get universal approbation'.[39] At an early meeting of the Blakeney Management Committee in 1913 it was agreed 'that having listened to all shades of opinion from the birdmen, not to advance further than public opinion in the locality was prepared to go'. Shooting should be by permit and only outside the breeding season, which lasted from the middle of May to mid-July.[40] Oliver supported the production of a 'descriptive pamphlet' to cover not only physical features, plants and animals but also the area's history, as 'the whole system of villages on Blakeney Harbour has had an interesting past'.[41] In fact, a series of booklets on different aspects of the natural history of the Point was produced and gathered into a single volume in 1952. This was edited by a second eminent academic who visited the Point regularly from the 1920s – the Cambridge-based coastal geomorphologist J.A. Steers. He regarded the Point as the prime research site in the country for the investigation of rates of salt-marsh accretion and tidal creek processes. Papers based on his research appeared regularly through the 1920s and 1930s.

By the outbreak of war in 1914 there was enough public concern to force the state to take the first tentative steps towards the protection of both wildlife and sites of historic and archaeological interest, and the state had recognised that it was appropriate to legislate to ensure this protection.

1   M. George (1992) *Landuse, ecology and conservation of Broadland*. Chichester, Packard, 449-50.
2   J. Roulett (1983) 'Late Victorian environmental organisations', *Victorian Studies* 26, 197-222.
3   Stevenson 1872, 7-19.
4   C.E. Gay (1944) 'Presidential address', *TNNNS* 16, 4 (In 1921 the NNNS took over the administration of these societies under the general title of the Norfolk Wild Bird Protection Society).
5    Letter to the *Eastern Daily Press*, 31 March 1921, 4.
6   NRO C/C 10/687.
7   M. Hunter (ed.) (1996) *Preserving the past: the rise of heritage in modern Britain*. Gloucester, Alan Sutton, 4.
8   PP 1841 437, Report of the Select Committee on National Monuments and Works of Art 1841, qu437, quoted in Hunter 1996, 40.

9    *Norfolk Archaeology* 6, 1859, passim.
10   J. Owen (2013) *Darwin's apprentice: an archaeological biography of John Lubbock*. Barnsley, Pen and Sword Archaeology, passim.
11   Quoted in P. Wright (2009) *On living in an old country*. Oxford, Oxford University Press, 45.
12   *The Times*, 13 April 1877, quoted by S. Thurley (2013) *Men from the ministry: how Britain saved its heritage*. Newhaven and London, Yale University Press, 39.
13   *Proceedings of the Society of Antiquaries* 9, 1881-3, 292, quoted in Saunders 1983, 11.
14   C.P. Kains-Jackson (1880) *Our ancient monuments and the land around them*. London, Elliot Stock.
15   M. Bowden (1991) *Pitt Rivers: the life and archaeological work of Lieutenant-General Pitt Rivers*, DCL, FRS, FSA. Cambridge, Cambridge University Press, 101.
16   *Report of the Inspector of Ancient Monuments 1912*, quoted in Saunders 1983, 18.
17   S. Fry (2013) 'Saving Britain's ancient sites', *British Archaeology* March/April, 30-35, 31.
18   Pitt-Rivers file FLO01551, quoted by Thurley 2013, 47.
19   J. Earl, 'London Government' in M. Hunter (ed.), *Preserving the past: the rise of heritage in modern Britain*. Gloucester, Alan Sutton, 61.
20   Saunders 1983, 11-33.
21   B.H. St J. O'Neil (1946) 'The Congress of Archaeological Societies', *Antiquaries Journal* 26, 61-6.
22   'Report for 1889', *Norfolk Archaeology* 11, 1892, ii.
23   B. Cowell (2008) *The heritage obsession: the battle for England's past*. Cirencester, Tempus, 99.
24   C. Mynors (2006) *Listed buildings, conservation areas and monuments*, 4th edn. London, Thomson, Sweet and Maxwell, 8-9.
25   P. Wade-Martins (1999) 'Discovering our past', in T. Heaton (ed.), *Norfolk century*, Norwich, *Eastern Daily Press*, 310.
26   Lowe 1989, 115.
27   A.G. Street (1937) 'The countryman's view', in C. Williams-Ellis (ed.), *Britain and the beast*, London, J.M. Dent, 122-32.
28   E.A. Ellis (1965) *The Broads*. London, Collins, xi; E. and R. Gurney (1908) The Sutton Freshwater Laboratory. No further details given; copy in Norfolk Heritage Centre, Norwich Central Library.
29   I. Rotherham (2013) *The lost fens: England's greatest ecological disaster*, London, The History Press, passim.
30   J. Sheail (1998) *Nature conservation in Britain*. London, HMSO, 3.
31   T.A. Rowell (1997) 'The history of the fen', in L. Friday (ed.) *Wicken Fen, the making of a wetland nature reserve*, London, Harley Books. 201-3.
32   M. Rothschild (1983) *Dear Lord Rothschild*. London, Hutchison, 89-93.
33   A.G. Tansley (ed.) (1911) *Types of British vegetation*. London, Central Committee for the Survey and Study of British Vegetation, 352-66.
34   Typescript at the Blakeney National Trust Office.
35   M. Waterson (2011) *A noble thing: the National Trust and its benefactors*. London, Scala Publishers, 139.
36   J. Sheail (1976) *Nature in trust*. Glasgow and London, Blaikie, 61 and 131.

37   F.W. Oliver (1913) *Journal of Ecology* 2, 'Nature Reserves' 55-56.

38   J. Sheail (2002) *Environmental history of the twentieth century*. Basingstoke, Palgrave, 124.

39   Typescript at the Blakeney National Trust Office.

40   Sheail 2002, 126.

41   Typescript at the Blakeney National Trust Office.

# 3

## The interwar years

Of all the schemes and ideas to preserve the animals and flowers — and indeed the scenery of England — I know of none that seems more quietly effective and more humane than those put in practice and fostered by the Norfolk Naturalists' Trust  (Sir William Beach Thomas, *The Spectator*, 27 June 1931)

In his reply Mr Bailey (of the National Trust) said 'He knew of no other county in England which had anything corresponding to the Norfolk Archaeological Trust...' (*The Times*, 8 September 1924)

The 1920s saw the setting up of two pioneering Trusts in Norfolk, one for wildlife and one for archaeological sites, of which one (the Naturalists' Trust) was to set the agenda for nature conservation in Norfolk for the rest of the century, in spite of the fact that, following the First World War, there was a stagnation in the study of botany. 'Was there less to discover? Or was it, as has been suggested, that more attention was now being paid to the budding science of ecology?'[1] 'Nature preservation failed to take off. Whether measured in terms of legislation, public awareness or nature reserves, the tangible achievements of the interwar years were meagre.'[2] If this analysis was true on the national stage, it certainly was not so in Norfolk, where an awareness of the fragility of the natural environment was clearly evident. The war years had resulted in the ploughing up of heath and the draining of marsh, and it was threats to the Cley Marshes from the War Agricultural Committee that led to concerns over its future and its purchase as a nature reserve.[3]

The period after 1918 saw immense change in the countryside, with increased tensions between the natural environment and man's activities. Improved roads, petrol stations, advertisement hoardings, electricity pylons and suburban sprawl were all seen as threats to the 'traditional countryside' and were themes taken up by many of the writers of the 1930s. 'When one considers the changes to the face of the county that are being made or are being contemplated by the Forestry Commission, the Drainage Boards, speculative builders and the like, one is anxious to preserve for future generations areas of marsh, heath, woods, and undrained fenland with their natural wealth of fauna and flora.'[4] The selling off of many of the great sporting estates, which had increasingly been managed for the protection of game, and the purchase of many farms by their tenants led to changes in land management, particularly the possibility that land that had previously been left for field sports would be brought into cultivation. However, as agricultural depression set in in the late 1920s the threat of the ploughing up of old pasture and thus the destruction of archaeological earthworks receded.

Concerns also came from another direction. The increasing availability of private transport in the form of the motor car meant that more people were able to visit what had previously been quiet 'unspoilt' areas, a situation bemoaned by nature lovers. After 1918 'beaches and quiet sea shore, up to this time known to comparatively few people interested in the birdlife there, were invaded by holidaymakers'.[5] The phrase 'beauty spot' entered the language, while the popularity of taking trips out into the country increased. Alongside the serious publications of botanists, ornithologists and antiquarians, this new interest in and nostalgia for the countryside was being fed by an ever-increasing number of popular books. From the 1930s Harry Batsford was producing a series of local guides. In 1939 *East Anglia*, for his 'Face of Britain' series, written by the Suffolk novelist Doreen Wallace, was published. Illustrations covered churches, great houses, rural scenes and picturesque villages and the author claimed to be 'a country woman with an eye for beauty' rather than an academic. The aim of such books, as Harry Batsford saw it, was to help urban dwellers to 'see the country — to get to understand, appreciate and realise something of the message of its outward aspect, its changing seasons, the people and their life and work'.[6] Arthur Mee's *King's England* series, describing counties village-by-village, began publication in the 1930s, with the Norfolk volume appearing in 1940. Described on the back cover as 'The indispensable companion of the Motor Age', it was read alongside the One-inch Ordnance Survey maps without which 'A holiday in any part of Great Britain is incomplete'. The publication of Roger Tory Petersen's *Field Guide* in 1934 provided for those with an interest in natural history and the countryside and gave a huge boost to the hobby of birdwatching.

While, in 1890, Pitt Rivers had worried about taxpayers' money being used to preserve ancient monuments of interest to only a very limited elite, such sites were now being visited by a far wider cross section of the public. Several Norfolk sites were taken into guardianship between the wars, with Castle Acre Priory being the first, in 1929.

Not only were more people visiting the countryside, but both public and private transport was enabling others to move out of the towns, thus invading the secluded surroundings of those who had come before. In spite of the complaints of those who had already escaped the towns, this exposure of the countryside to a wider audience did have the positive affect of increasing people's awareness of both the natural world and the historic interest of their surroundings.

## Interwar Broadland and Breckland

It was the period after the First World War which saw the real explosion of the Broadland holiday industry. While there were 165 boats available for hire in the Broads in 1920, by 1939 there were 587 and in 1955, 919.[7] The popularity of sailing on the Broads impacted on the landscape of the area generally, but particularly on those villages with railway stations such as Wroxham, Horning, Hoveton, Brundall and Potter Heigham. Here ease of access was combined with wooded and undulating scenery that added a picturesque quality which was lacking nearer Yarmouth[8] – or, as the guide book put it when describing Wroxham:

*19  Castle Acre Priory, taken into Guardianship in 1929,
shown as it was before it was taken over and as it is now.*

A joyous spot and beautiful, with a charm shared by no other holiday centre in the kingdom; the rural approach to much that is most fascinating in this region of out-of-the-world enchantment ... a stepping stone to a magic realm where there is no movement save that of the water and the swaying reeds and no sound but the cry of the wild birds.[9]

Boatyards flourished, building, maintaining and hiring out boats. Hotels and guesthouses, regarded by some as 'unsightly modern houses for accommodation of visitors', sprang up.[10] Holiday houses and villas, from the grandest to the most simple Boulton and Paul prefabricated and corrugated iron bungalows, or even home-made constructions, appeared along the banks, and there was plenty of opportunity for the conservationists in their tudoresque brick houses to grumble about the railway carriages and 'shacks' put up by those humbler folk who enjoyed a bit of coarse fishing on a day off.

The railway not only allowed holidaymakers ease of access but meant that wealthy Norwich families could afford to leave the city and live permanently in the countryside. One of the finest houses resulting from these developments is that at How Hill (now a residential educational centre), perfectly sited overlooking the River Ant, designed by the influential Norwich architect Edward Boardman and built between 1901 and 1903. Thatched and built of roughcast brick to give a vernacular feel, its detailing is Jacobean. It was those people who owned these substantial riverside villas who were most likely to complain about the increasing numbers and changing types of 'trippers', a term always used in a derogatory way. They were blamed, for example, for substantial damage to the stonework of St Benet's Abbey in 1928,[11] but the conflicts over development and use of the Broads were often as much about class as conservation.

It is clear that the different strands of the holiday industry affected the landscape in different ways, from the large Edwardian hotels to the caravan and holiday camps, and all were seen as a threat to the natural and historic landscape. It is also clear that the expanding availability of transport to the countryside meant that, while the rural population was declining, a far wider cross section of the population was coming into contact with the countryside and taking an interest in changes taking place; its recreational as well as its food-producing role was beginning to be of concern to more than the landed gentry. A newspaper article of 1920 stressed the value of commons not only to the local inhabi-

20 *Perhaps the most impressive of the holiday homes built in the Broads is How Hill House in Ludham. It was built by the architect Edward Boardman between 1903 and 1905 and perfectly sited with views over the River Ant and the Reedham marshes.*

tants but also to those from the towns: 'It is generally admitted that common lands are not only important as a means of livelihood for the small holder and others who live upon their boundaries, but also as a source of fresh air and recreation for the town dwellers.'[12]

It was not only those with cars who bought guide books of the kind being produced from the 1930s. A good network of buses running from the train

21 *Most of the manual planting of over 2,000 acres a year of conifers by the Forestry Commission was undertaken by unemployed labour from the north of England during the 1930s. Here nursery beds of young conifers are being inspected in the 1950s.*

stations in many a market town as well as the bicycle allowed urban dwellers to explore the countryside, its churches, village greens and pubs. Camping holidays also became fashionable, with cyclists and walkers bringing their tents, often in small hand carts or pulled behind their bicycles. Hiking became popular in the 1920s and 1930s, with the Ramblers' Association being founded in 1935. By the 1930s troops of Boy Scouts came out from the towns and, having introduced themselves to the local vicar, would ask permission to camp in a farmer's field. Some campers were not so considerate, however. Having complained about those who pitched tents without permission, left gates open and dropped litter, a correspondent to the *Eastern Daily Press* went on to say 'I am confident that any Norfolk farmer would accede to any reasonable request which would pro-mote the enjoyment of holiday-makers, but it is not fair to expect us to suffer fools gladly.'[13]

As early as 1884 G.C. Davies' description of a village on the River Yare was of a scene that visitors expected to see and which they associated with an 'unchanging' countryside.

From a grey stone bridge we see an old-fashioned village, built with delightful irregularity, the houses with strange and fantastically curved gables. Through the village runs the broad high road to the city ... a little apart on the banks of the river stands the hoary church.[14]

What life was like for the villagers in their tumbledown gabled cottages was of little concern to those enjoying the quaint view.

Alongside the increasing popularity of the Broads went a concern for the future of Breckland, which was being threatened from a different direction. As a result of timber shortages in the First World War the government adopted a policy of afforestation. In 1919 Forestry Acts authorised the appointment of Forestry Commissioners who were empowered to acquire land. Several contributory factors combined to create a unique situation enabling the purchase of land for forestry. At this time of agricultural depression poor land was cheap to buy and the country's wood supplies, depleted by wartime requirements, needed replenishing. There was also a need to find employment for the unemployed, and work in tree planting was seen as one solution. The sandy soils of Breckland were highly suited to forestry and from 1922 the Commission began buying land in the area, with nearly 15,000 acres purchased by 1925. Both arable and heathland rapidly gave way to conifer plantation, with an average of 1,300 acres being planted every year between 1922 and 1960, the bulk of it in the first decade, with 2,226 acres planted annually between 1924 and 1929.[15] At 40,000 acres, Thetford Forest is the largest lowland forest in Britain. In 1880 there had been 54,000 acres of heathland in the Norfolk and Suffolk Breckland, but by 1968 only 6,600 remained.[16] Just as Breckland began to disappear, its unique qualities were being recognised. In 1925 W.G. Clarke's *In Breckland wilds* was published and immediately became a classic. In describing the natural and geological history of the heaths, using words such as 'spaciousness' and 'peaceful solitude' to describe the area, Clarke exudes an enthusiasm for the Brecks which is infectious. 'He who has vibrated with the thrill of the heathland is never quite the same again.'[17] The popularity of such books is an indication of the widening interest in the countryside and a growing awareness of its fragility away from the standard holiday resorts.

## The role of the National Trust

After its initial acquisitions on the north coast the Trust was nervous of acquiring more sites and lengthy negotiations were needed before they took on land neighbouring Blakeney Point at Scolt Head. This was bought from Lord Leicester with funds raised through the efforts of Oliver and Sydney Long, a Wells doctor and honorary secretary of the NNNS. An undated letter preserved at Holkham from Dr Frank Penrose, who presented two 'rare migrants', a barrell warbler and a lecterine warbler, to Lord Leicester for his collection, reads 'I am sure all naturalists are most grateful to you for what you have done in saving Scolt Head and the Burnham Overy Marshes.'[18] The area was finally handed over to the National Trust in 1923 'so that it could be preserved for ever as a nature reserve'. A watcher's hut from which the terneries could be guarded from egg collectors and other disturbance was designed in an arts and crafts style by the Norwich architect Edward Boardman.[19] In 1937 the foreshore off Scolt Head was acquired from the Board of Trade. A further site acquired in the 1930s from the Felbrigg estate was over 60 acres of West Runton Common.

A further important acquisition of the National Trust in Norfolk, which was again a first, was the gift of Blickling Hall along with 4,270 acres of land from the Marquis of Lothian (1882–1940).[20] As the son of Lord Ralph Kerr, the third son of the seventh Marquis of Lothian had a traditional aristocratic upbringing on the family estate at Newbattle, near Edinburgh. After Oxford he spent four and a half years in South Africa working for Lord Milner on plans to rebuild the colony following the Boer War. Here his earnestness, coupled with a strong sense of duty, was obvious and would ensure that he would always be an influential figure in government circles. It also convinced him of the value of the British Empire as a world-wide force for good and he travelled widely, lecturing to encourage a spirit of cooperation among its members. To this end he became editor of a quarterly review of imperial politics. All of these made him an expert in foreign and imperial affairs, but travelling and the intensity which he gave to his work resulted in a nervous breakdown in 1913, after which he joined the Astor family in St Moritz for a long rest. As secretary to Lloyd George from 1916 to 1922 he attended the 1919 Versailles peace conference. A charming and good-looking man, a golfer with a love of motorbikes in his youth — later replaced by fast cars

22  *Above: the Watcher's hut on Scolt Head was designed by Edward Boardman in an arts and crafts style soon after Scolt Head was taken over by the National Trust in 1923. Below: The Scolt Head Committee outside the Watcher's hut, June 1928.*

— he played a not insignificant role in great international affairs, yet never became pompous. Although not closely aligned to any political party his views tended to coincide with those of the Liberals. He felt that responsibility was the sole justification for privilege and power and, in principle, he supported Lloyd George's tax reforms: 'In my capacity as an ordinary citizen I think highly of these arrangements, but as an inheritor of a title and estates thereto they will prove somewhat embarrassing.'[21] This proved to be the case when, on the death of his father in 1930, he inherited the title of tenth Lord Lothian and three fine houses and their estates, bringing with them death duties of £300,000 which could be paid only by selling some of most valuable books from the Blickling library. This made him very aware of the effect a further round of death duties would have on the estate. In 1930 he wrote to *The Times* urging that income from death duties should be used to support agriculture, and he then became a spokesman for the National Trust. Up to this date its experiences of taking on large country houses had been financial disasters. Under new leadership, however, the Trust, still a small organisation with a membership of little over 3,000, was ready to embark on new acquisition policies. At the 1934 Annual General Meeting Lord Lothian gave a speech entitled 'England's Country Houses: the case for their preservation', arguing that the main threat came from the level of death duties. The solution, as he saw it, was for the National Trust to take over properties without any burden of taxation and this eventually became law under the National Trust Act of 1937. The act enabled the Trust to hold land and investments free of tax as endowments for country houses. In future, whole estates could be given to the Trust without incurring tax liabilities. The Act also allowed for the furniture and pictures within the house to be excluded from valuation for taxation.

Lord Lothian died in 1940 while British ambassador in Washington and left the Blickling estate, with its 100 cottages, to the National Trust, making it the first of many country house acquisitions to benefit from the 1937 Act. Of his other houses, Newbattle had been given to the University of Edinburgh as an adult education college, Ferniehurst, a border castle overlooking the River Jed, was let at a small rent to the Scottish Youth Hostel Association, while the modern house at Monteviot remained in family occupation.

Blickling, however, was his favourite and although his public and diplomatic duties left him little time to enjoy it he hoped that, under National Trust owner-

*23 Blickling Hall, with its surrounding estate, was the first to be gifted to the National Trust by Lord Lothian under the Country Houses Scheme in 1940.*

ship, it would become not a 'melancholy museum' but set 'a standard of beauty, in garden and furniture and decoration by which later generations can mould their own practice'.[22] In 1952 Oxburgh Hall was acquired by the National Trust under a similar arrangement.

## The Royal Society for the Protection of Birds

During most of the interwar period the RSPB was more concerned with lobbying for improved legislation to protect birds than the acquisition of sites. A major concern of the 1920s was the damage caused to sea birds by oil spillages, but any attempts to control the emptying of bilge tanks needed international agreement. The society continued to call for one and publicised the need. Finally, in 1926, a meeting took place in Washington, but it ended without agreement and all the RSPB could do was call for voluntary agreements, in which it was partially successful.

## Two local Trusts

Norfolk is remarkable in that the 1920s saw the founding of two local trusts with the aim of acquiring and conserving sites of wildlife and historical interest. Both of these were founded and promoted by a small group of local natural historians and antiquarians, many of them landed gentry and eminent in their fields. The Norfolk Archaeological Trust (NAT) was founded in 1923 and the Norfolk Naturalists' Trust (NNT) in 1926. Pivotal to both trusts in their early days was the support of the Norwich solicitor Basil Cozens-Hardy (1885–1976) and, early on, both trusts held their committee meetings in the offices of Cozens-Hardy and Jewson at Castle Chambers in Opie Street. Basil was a remarkable man. Very tall, and of impressive build, he had lost a leg while a pilot in the First World War. This did not cramp his style, however. He had a metallic artificial leg and kept a few spare in a cupboard in the offices – 'a somewhat unnerving sight' for junior staff. He is said to have ridden a bicycle and stories of how he mounted it were told from time to time. During the interwar years he played cricket for Norfolk with the help of a runner.[23] As a member of the Cozons Hardy family of Letheringsett he was very well connected within the county, being on the committee of many city charities as well as the Board of Norwich Union. He was made a Deputy Lord Lieutenant in 1935, when he was also Sheriff of Norwich. The family had many influential friends. Basil describes in his diary the visit of his school friend Augustus Birrell to the family home in Letheringsett in 1912, when he was Chief

24 *Basil Cozons-Hardy was the founder of the Norfolk Archaeological Trust and was influential in the Naturalists' Trust. This civic portrait shows him in 1935 as Sheriff of Norwich.*

Secretary for Ireland. 'He was accompanied by a detective to guard against the suffragettes.' Like so many of the early supporters of local charities and trusts, Basil was a nonconformist; while he lived in Norwich he supported the large Congregational chapel just around the corner from Castle Chambers, in Princes Street. After the death of his father he moved back to the family home in Letheringsett and his funeral was held in the Methodist church in neighbouring Holt.

## *The Norfolk Archaeological Trust (NAT)*

Basil had joined the Norfolk and Norwich Archaeological Society (NNAS) in 1919 and within three years he was Excursion Secretary. It was this role which enabled him to become familiar with archaeological sites across the county and this knowledge was put to good use when he recommended sites for scheduling as protected ancient monuments. He could see that the NNAS was not a suitable body for the owning of property and so founded the NAT as an independent trust closely linked to the Society. Its aims, stated in its Memorandum and Articles, were 'to promote and foster the discovery, excavation, preservation,

25 *The clearance of the site at Binham Priory was carried out by the Ministry of Works in 1932-39. The work was done with little concern for the archaeological layers, but rather in preparation for its opening to the public (left).*
*Above: Binham Priory as it is today.*

recording and study of sites and objects of archaeological importance within the county of Norfolk for the public benefit'. This stress on preservation was revolutionary at a time when excavation and the collecting of objects was the main aim of many archaeologists. It was a cause taken up by O.G.S. Crawford, who pioneered the use of aerial photography to discover archaeological sites and who, in 1920, was appointed archaeological officer to the Ordnance Survey. Six years after the founding of NAT he wrote in the editorial of the first volume of *Antiquity*: 'conservation, not excavation is the need of the day'.[24] The first meeting of the NAT was held in the Norfolk and Norwich Library in March 1923. It was agreed that the Council should consist of not less than ten and not more than twenty and the original members included the Indian prince and antiquarian Duleep Singh as vice-president and Basil Cozens-Hardy as secretary. The Norwich architect William Boardman and W.G. Clarke, better known as the author of *In Breckland Wilds*, were both council members. The first site which concerned the new Trust was drawn to its attention by the Runton Common Purchase Fund, which wanted to preserve the common with its 'Roman Camp' (in fact a Napoleonic War beacon site) as an open space. Ten guineas was granted to the fund on the understanding that the Trust would be given a mandate to manage the beacon. Having raised the money the common was then given to the National Trust, but the NAT maintained an interest in its management and owned several strips within it until 1969, when the whole area became a registered common and there was no longer any need to retain a token ownership.

More important was the purchase in October 1924 of the Augustine Steward's House, a fine mid-sixteenth-century timber-framed building on Tombland. It had been put up for sale along with the neighbouring Samson and Hercules building in Norwich, which had then to be sold on. A joint appeal with the Archaeological Society was needed to raise the necessary money, and an overdraft was required to cover the 'preservation work'.

In 1932 Binham Priory was the first archaeological monument to be purchased by the Trust, with the help of £279 raised by a public appeal, leaving only a small balance to be found. The site was immediately handed over to the Ministry of Works (now English Heritage) to manage in guardianship. As was usual with properties newly acquired by the Office of Works, clearance of the site in preparation for opening to the public took place. The ground level of the field was lowered as the floor levels of the priory were revealed. However, much of the work was undertaken by workmen with little archaeological supervision. There was no proper report written and, although some of the finds were kept, there is no plan showing where they were found. This type of excavation or 'clearance' was typical of the period and has generated long-lasting criticism from archaeologists of later and more methodical generations. At the time it was believed in scholarly circles that the results of excavation would add little to the dating and understanding of documented medieval sites.[25]

The 1920s saw increasing concern over the future of windmills and there were efforts by the NAT to find one that might be suitable for purchase and conservation. Protracted negotiations for Sprowston Mill began in 1926, but were brought to an abrupt end when it was burnt down in 1933. The Trust was actively seeking buildings to buy through the late 1920s and 1930s. Pykerells House in St Mary's Plain, Norwich, a late-fifteenth-century hall-house and one of only seven thatched buildings remaining in the city, was bought in 1928 for £350. The building had been the house of Thomas Pykerell, Lord Mayor of Norwich, in 1525, 1533 and 1538 and had a fine oriel hall window and queen post roof with elaborately carved spandrels. A lease was negotiated for the redundant St Peter Hungate church, also in Norwich, in 1931.

In Kings Lynn the seventeenth-century timber-framed and jettied merchant's house known as the Greenland Fisheries Museum was bought in 1932 from the executors of Edward Beloe, one of the original signatories of the Trust's Memorandum and articles. With the help of an honourary curator the museum was reopened in 1936. However, the building was badly damaged during the war and the museum exhibits handed over to the Kings Lynn Corporation. The building was then repaired and let as a house.

In 1929 the Trust took on a lease of Bishop Bonner's Cottages, a row of seventeenth-century timber-framed cottages in Dereham with fine pargetting along the front and a cruck roof, and finally bought them in 1939. In 1954 they were leased to the Dereham and District Antiquarian Society. Without the Trust becoming involved these cottages would probably have been pulled down for road widening.

A letter circulated to members in 1936 stated that 'with the rapid development of modern buildings … we are anxious to preserve and keep in good condition

THIS HOUSE
purchased and preserved in 1924 by the
Norfolk Archæological Trust was built by
AUGUSTINE STEWARD, Mercer.
Sheriff 1526, Mayor 1534; 1546 and 1556
Burgess in Parliament 1547.

*26  Properties purchased by the
Norfolk Archaeological Trust in the
1920s and 1930s included (top and
above) Augustine Stewards House,
Tombland; (right) Bishop Bonner's
Cottages, East Dereham; (opposite,
top) Greenland Fisheries, Kings
Lynn; (below, left) a seventeenth-
century cottage in Field Dalling;
(below right) Pykerell's house,
St Mary's Plain, Norwich.*

typical cottages and buildings of olden days in various parts of the County'. True to this aim, in 1938 a 'picturesque seventeenth century cottage in Field Dalling' was added to the Trust's portfolio. It can be seen that the emphasis at this time was very much on buildings rather than the more general sites and objectives specified at its foundation. It was not until much later that the preservation of archaeological sites became an important consideration. However, the lack of membership and thus of funds was a continuing problem, and appeals to members of the Archaeological Society did not produce results. Considering the small size of its membership, the Trust's achievements in its early years were impressive.[26]

## The Norfolk Naturalists' Trust

A similar need for the preservation of wildlife sites of importance was recognised in 1926, when the Norfolk Naturalists' Trust (NNT) was set up independently of the Norfolk and Norwich Naturalists' Society (NNNS) with the specific aim of procuring land to create nature reserves. Following the purchase of Blakeney Point in 1912, Scolt Head was bought from Lord Leicester in 1926 and, like Blakeney Point, handed over to the National Trust. However, there were already those who felt that local sites should be managed through a local rather than a national trust. The prime mover in this was Dr Sydney Long (1870–1939), the son of a Wells doctor who was familiar from childhood with the salt marshes. His working life was spent as a doctor in Norwich, where he was a well-respected physician at both the Norfolk and Norwich and Jenny Lind hospitals. His main fields of activity were ornithology and entomology and, in particular, the theory which had been proposed by Sir Ronald Ross that malaria could be carried by mosquitoes. This was of local relevance in that 'Fen ague', associated with fens and marshes, was also a form of malaria. However, Dr Long's lifelong interest was in ornithology and he spent his leisure out in his open-topped car, recording in detailed diaries in a meticulous hand numerous sightings of birds and their activities. Like so many naturalists before him he lived in Surrey Street in Norwich, within easy reach of the hospital.

As well as being an academic and active researcher, he was a great organiser.

*27 Dr Sydney Long (1870–1939), founder of the Norfolk Naturalists' Trust. He is shown here at Scolt Head.*

*28 The Cley marshes were the first acquisition of the Norfolk Naturalists' Trust in 1926. The scrapes to attract waders have been dug recently and the new Visitor Centre can be seen in the bottom right-hand corner.*

When, in 1921, the four Norfolk Bird Protection Societies amalgamated, he became their honorary secretary and initiated some exemplary prosecutions of predatory collectors of rare birds and their eggs.[27] At different times he was both secretary and president of the NNNS as well as the editor of its journal, which under his control reached a high academic standard. His two interests in medicine and ornithology were shared by the Duke of Bedford, who carried on a detailed correspondence with him between 1914 and 1923 about the birds he had seen as well as the layout and management of the hospital he supported on his estates.[28]

Long was well aware that the NNNS was an academic society, unsuited to the owning of land. He had been a prime mover in raising the funds for the purchase of Scolt Head and was a member of the Blakeney Point Local Management

Committee. He had observed the National Trust's reluctance to overstretch itself and when, in March 1926, 407 acres of the Cley marshes plus a building plot came on the market, Long purchased it himself. Frustrated by the procrastination of the National Trust, he then invited a group of like-minded individuals to a lunch in Cley to consider the setting up of a Naturalists' Trust so that the marshes could be vested in the hands of, and administered by, local naturalists. As a result, the NNT was formed as a company limited by guarantee. The aims in the Memorandum of Association, under 24 headings, were deliberately wide. The most significant were 'To protect places and objects of natural beauty or of ornithological, botanical, geological or scientific interest from injury, ill treatment or destruction', to 'establish ... reserves' and to accept subscriptions. The membership should not exceed 200 and life membership was £10.

The first meeting of the Trust was on 30 November 1926 in the solicitors' offices of Cozens-Hardy and Jewson, and their Castle Chambers was to be the registered office. Others present included such well-known names as R.J. Colman and G.H. Gurney, as well as Dr Long. Surprisingly, after some discussion, shooting out of the breeding season at Cley continued to be allowed, perhaps because C. Mclean, who was also a member of the shooting syndicate, was present. A new five-year agreement with the syndicate, at £225 per annum, was agreed. The grazing tenancies on the marsh would continue, but were rearranged so that the central part was reserved for nesting birds. Twenty-six life members (all from the local gentry) were admitted. The first AGM was held at the Castle Museum in February 1927, when the accounts were presented and agreed.[29]

The main concern of the early conservationists was the north Norfolk coast, with its marshes. Salt marshes tended to be dismissed by the romantic admirers of the 'picturesque' as flat, bleak and inhospitable. However, their importance for breeding and migrating birds was critical. In 1929 a house at Brancaster Staithe was acquired and in 1937 the adjoining cottage was bought to extend visitor facilities. In 1937 the Duchess of Bedford gave land at Burnham Overy Staithe, while Little Eye and Great Eye at Salthouse were bought in 1937 with the help of a grant from the Pilgrim Trust. These areas of coastal marshland offered some of the best vantage points for observing migrating and wading birds.

The Broads were, as we have seen, vulnerable to disturbance by tourists. However, they were mostly in the hands of sympathetic owners. In March 1929 the NNT purchased marshland at Martham from Norfolk County Council for £150, and in 1930 fourteen acres of reed bed and twenty acres of arable and marsh at Alderfen Broad was bought, helped by an interest-free loan from Major Trafford of Wroxham Hall. In 1946 Sir Christopher Cadbury helped the Trust to buy the Whiteslea estate at Hickling, where he had the use of the house, while in 1949 Ranworth and Cockshoot Broad were given to the trust by Colonel Cator subject to the king having one day's shooting a year.[30]

In addition to the north Norfolk Coast and the Broads, a third area of important habitats was Breckland, which was subject to different pressures. Here the Forestry Commission was regarded as a threat to the heathland environment. It was with great difficulty that the NNT finally managed to obtain land there. In March 1932 Dr Long reported that, although he had made enquiries, he had not heard of any part of Breckland which could be acquired for the Trust. His only suggestion was the purchase of cottages with commoning rights in Lakenheath, which would ensure that Lakenheath Common could not be planted, and these were bought in 1933. This failed to secure the common, however, as the land was taken over as an airfield early in the war. Protracted negotiations began in 1938 for land at Wretham. The Forestry Commission had recently purchased a large area of Breckland around Wretham and Kilverstone and agreed to sell that around Wretham Hall to Mrs Riches, who planned to give it 'as a sanctuary for all time' to the NNT in memory of her father, Sir John Dewrance. Lord Fisher of Kilverstone would also contribute land and part of the mere if he could keep the duck shooting, but Mrs Riches refused to purchase the land from the Forestry Commission if this was part of the bargain. Finally 500 acres was handed over to the NNT, but, again, some had to be handed on to the Ministry of Defence for military training as part of the Battle Area and for an airfield. Attempts to protect further areas from afforestation continued, with the acquisition of 260 acres at Weeting. This land was important not only as a potential nature reserve and bird sanctuary but also as an archaeological site, as the heath contained several barrows. This purchase was made possible by a gift of £900 from Christopher Cadbury, who had moved to Norwich in 1939 to manage the family's chocolate-making business. He was to become an important benefactor of the NNT as well as a prime mover in the conservation movement nationally. Not only did he have wealth at his disposal but he was a great committee man, working for both

29  In the early days of the Norfolk Wildlife Trust a major source of
income was the sale of Christmas cards. These examples are from
1958 and 1959.

national parks and national nature reserves as well as the RSPB and the World Wildlife Fund. He was a founder member of the Royal Society of Wildlife Trusts, which coordinated the work of local bodies such as the NNT. In 1945 he was coopted onto the NNT Council and remained a member for forty-three years. In 1949 he bought 225 acres of Thetford Heath – 'typical rabbit-cropped stoney breck of which so little survives in a natural form' – which he then gave to the NNT.[31]

It would have come as a surprise to the early naturalists that in recent years Thetford Forest has been designated as a Site of Special Scientific Interest (SSSI) and a Specially Protected Area (SPA) (a European designation) because of the unique habitat it provides for birds such as the woodlark and nightjar. As timber has been thinned out from twenty years of growth to final felling at sixty years, natural regeneration of native trees has taken place and a millennium forest scheme covering 300 acres of heathland in six different lots has been created and managed by the NWT, thus finally allowing it to achieve the aim of its founders. The diversity of conifers and deciduous trees alongside open heath has created an environment suited to a wide variety of wildlife, including the rare stone curlew. Under the shelter of the pines, plants adapted to hostile conditions can survive.

In its early years the NNT restricted membership to 200, with a subscription of £10 securing a life membership. In the years leading to the outbreak of war membership grew to 150. More sites were acquired, so that by 1939 the Trust owned land worth over £14,000. In 1939 it was able to appoint a secretary and assistant treasurer at a salary of £300 a year plus a £20 car allowance. The largest source of income for the Trust was the sale of Christmas cards. Taking the idea from the RSPB, who had been selling cards and calenders from 1899, it was made possible by the gift every year from 1930 of a painting of a bird by the eminent wildlife artist F.C. Harrison. His picture was used for the card and then auctioned. By 1939 40,000 were sold each year. Within two years of its purchase in 1930, the overdraft on Alderfen Broad had been paid off entirely from the sale of Christmas cards.

30 *Ted Ellis (1910-1986). As keeper of Natural History in the Norwich Castle Museum in the 1930s, and later through his weekly columns in the Eastern Daily Press, Ted Ellis became the public face of natural history and conservation within the county.*

## Ted Ellis

Alongside the important work of the Trusts in bringing the causes of conservation to the public went the influence of individuals. Ted Ellis (1910-1986) became the public face of Norfolk's natural history between the wars. Writing a weekly column in the *Eastern Daily Press* for forty years from 1928, he described the world of the Norfolk fens and waterways and emphasised the need for their protection and conservation. By 1930 he was working firstly in the Tollhouse Museum in Yarmouth and then in the Castle Museum in Norwich, where, as keeper of

natural history, he initiated the installation of a new and much more lively type of exhibit than the glass cases of stuffed birds and animals he found on his arrival. These were the three-dimensional displays known as dioromas in which wildlife was shown in its natural setting. He commissioned the building of several pieces with backgrounds painted by well-known theatre artists, Owen Paul Smyth and Ernest Whately, each illustrating the environment and wildlife of the regions of Norfolk, including the Broads, the Brecks, the coast and a Norfolk 'loke' or lane. The museum curator of the time, Frank Leney, described them as 'exhibits of extreme beauty and interest' which will 'attract wide attention and stimulate the desire to protect and preserve the wildlife which still survives in Norfolk'. They were installed between 1931 and 1936 in what was called the Norfolk Room (now the Ted Ellis Room), and they are still some of the most popular exhibits in the museum. Ellis also initiated an ambitious card index record (the foundation of the current Biological Record) covering every species of plant and

31 *These dioramas in the Norfolk Room at the Castle Museum were the brainchild of Ted Ellis. Those illustrated here show Breckland with a stone curlew in the foreground, a broadland scene with a crested grebe, and Breydon Water with a bird of prey — all shown within their natural surroundings and a great contrast to the rows of stuffed birds in glass cases of an earlier era.*

animal known in Norfolk, noting where it had been seen, when, how often and by whom. In 1946 he bought and moved to 150 acres at Wheatfen, near Surlingham. He became a popular broadcaster and writer in the 1950s and 1960s, urging vigilant care of the natural beauty of the region. After his death in 1987 Wheatfen was established as a permanent nature reserve.[32]

## Rainbird Clarke

Overlapping with Ellis for a few years at the Castle Museum was Rainbird Clarke (1914-1963). The son of W.G. Clarke, he continued his father's work of recording archaeological sites. From the 1930s onwards, initially for the Ordnance Survey, he started to build up a record of antiquities shown on their maps. This developed into a card index of archaeological discoveries which forms the basis of the modern computerised Historic Environment Record. While at the Castle Museum he initiated several excavations and his book *East Anglia*, published in 1960, was the first modern systematic account of the archaeology of the region.[33]

## The beginnings of national pressure groups: the Society for the Promotion of Nature Reserves

Pressure groups such as the RSPB, whose early campaigns in the 1890s had been against the import of exotic bird feathers for ladies' hats, had existed before 1918, but it was after that date that threats to the environment seemed more pressing. New groups were formed and older ones became more active. The Society for the Promotion of Nature Reserves (SPNR), set up in 1912, was influenced by the new science of ecology and the understanding of causal relationships between habitats and animal and plant communities. Its foundation by Charles Rothschild had been greeted by a leader in *The Times* bewailing the fact that, while the nineteenth century had seen a drift away from the countryside, the improvements in transport were seeing a move back from the towns. The risk was that the entire countryside would be covered by 'a sort of universal suburb'.[34] This may seem rather an exaggeration at this time, and the Society's aim of creating a list

32 *Rainbird Clarke (1914–1963) was curator of the Norwich Castle Museum and responsible for establishing a record of archaeological sites which became the foundation of the modern Historic Environment Record (HER).*

of nationally important sites that should be protected as nature reserves was not fully appreciated by the mainstream nature conservation movement. Bodies such as the RSPB were more concerned with promoting legislation against bird catching and egg collecting, and nature reserves were seen as of less importance and very expensive. The Society's work, however, became urgent as the First World War progressed and the Board of Agriculture produced a list of areas of land, including uncultivated marshes and heaths, that the Board felt were suitable for ploughing as part of the war effort. A provisional list of 251 sites, including fifty-two classed as the most important, was sent to the Board in June 1915. This included the north Norfolk coast around Burnham Overy, the Norfolk Broads and Winterton on the east coast.

Professor Oliver, who had been a member of the SPNR executive Committee from 1912, expressed the view at the first meeting of the British Ecological Society in 1913 that 'the country districts of England are not obviously seriously threatened and therefore the nature reserve movement does not have strong popular appeal', especially as nature reserves were seen as areas which, rather like game reserves, would restrict public access.[35] At a meeting of the British Association in Leeds in 1927 which discussed the role of nature reserves, Oliver again stressed the importance of the SPNR, pointing to the 'revolution in communications which petrol and the motor car had wrought' and thus the urgent need for obtaining representative examples of natural ground with its flora and fauna, so that these might serve as 'present enjoyment and solace and might be handed down to future generations intact'. In this he thought that local trusts such as the NNT should play a vital role.[36] However, it was many years before any other county Trusts came into being, and the SPNR achieved little in the years following Charles Rothschild's death in 1923.

## The beginnings of national pressure groups: the Council for the Preservation of Rural England

Conservation in the interwar years was concerned not only with the protection of individual sites of natural or antiquarian interest but also with the preservation of the wider countryside. The Council for the Preservation (later changed to Protection) of Rural England (CPRE) was founded nationally in the same year as the NNT (1926) with a much wider remit – to preserve 'all things of value and beauty'. The man behind the CPRE, which consisted of a small group of London-centred intellectuals, was the architect and town planner Patrick Abercrombie. He saw that the countryside was being affected by rapid and damaging change, and that the protection of both the countryside and the coast was needed. The CPRE's aim was to encourage the preservation of 'all things of true value and beauty, and the scientific and orderly development of all local resources'. It was very much an aesthetic movement, with a deep antipathy towards industrialisation, and saw the future of the countryside in the revitalising of farming. Its concern was the countryside as a whole, rather than individual sites, and particularly the unplanned scruffy sprawl of new housing development. This included the 'holiday shacks' in the Broads. CPRE policy was never to own property, but rather to act as a pressure group to influence owners, public opinion and local authorities. A plan to buy land on the coast at Stiffkey to protect it from further invasion by the War Department in 1939 was mooted, but doomed to failure. The Norfolk branch was founded in November 1933, well after many of the groups in other counties. Its stated aim was 'to guide necessary development upon right and orderly lines, so that our great heritage may be handed on unimpaired'. The heritage the CPRE wished to protect included the city of Norwich and the port of Kings Lynn, the Norfolk Broads — 'a unique landscape in the British Isles' — picturesque villages and churches. The earl of Leicester supported the founding of a county branch and spoke of the 'unsightly bungalow development on the important salt marsh coast from Sandringham to Sheringham'. A dislike of this type of development was frequently voiced. For instance, Mr Bristow of Hunstanton wrote to the London office of the CPRE complaining about the development along the Kings Lynn Road 'of the commonist type of bungalow'.[37] Early in 1934 a provisional local committee was formed to discuss a constitution and committee structure. The original committee included several landowners, such as the historian R.W. Ketton-Cremer of Felbrigg, Roger Coke of Bayfield, Captain Desmond Buxton of Catton and Alec Penrose of Bradenham. Perhaps we should not be surprised that Basil Cozens-Hardy was also an active committee member.[38] On many occasions the CPRE worked hand-in-hand with both the NNT and the National Trust. In 1937 a scheme for the management of the Morston and Stiffkey marshes was promoted by the CPRE whereby covenants with the National Trust would be entered into by the owners. All three bodies were working in 'friendly co-operation'.[39] Early campaigns of the CPRE included criticism of local landowners for felling and selling the limited timber left on their estates, drawing attention to the problems of litter, road widening, demolition of old cottages and barns, and ribbon development. The County Council was asked to stop digging road material from the coastal hills behind Morston and agreed to do so. At the CPRE AGM of 1938 there was already concern about the loss of hedgerows and the effects on the countryside of increasing farm mechanisation. Problems which conservationists of all types still face were thus already evident in the interwar years. How could the countryside be protected while promoting its appreciation by a wider public? Could it be protected from urban influence while making it more accessible?[40]

## National parks

One solution to this problem was seen as the creation of national parks, of which the original list of proposed sites included the Norfolk Broads. Agitation, supported by the CPRE, had begun in the 1920s and led to the appointment of the Addison Committee to investigate the need for national parks. A Standing Committee on National Parks, set up in 1936, attempted to coordinate the often conflicting interests of the amenity societies who campaigned for more public access and the nature conservationists who wanted to protect nature reserves from visitors. While there were those who felt that these two aims were incompatible, it was the firm belief of the Committee's first chairman, John Dower, that recreation and conservation must come together for the common good, but in spite of the presentation of a draft National Parks Bill in 1939, nothing was achieved before the outbreak of war.

## The role of local and national government

The interwar period also saw the beginning of powers over planning and conservation being granted to local authorities. The 1929 Local Government Act encouraged the setting up of planning committees covering several rural and urban district councils to advise on planning issues. The first in East Anglia was the Norfolk (East Central) Joint Planning Committee in 1930. That for the north and east followed in 1934. Their responsibilities included the drawing up of planning schemes for their area and advising the local councils. The zoning of industrial and commercial development as well as the safeguarding of natural characteristics was seen as of prime importance. The north and east committee, which covered part of the Broads, advised that the river banks and land near the Broads should be kept in their natural state, areas of special landscape value should be preserved and there should be strict control on the design and external appearance of buildings.[41]

## The Office of Works

The Ancient Monuments Act of 1913 had seen the beginning of a realistic approach to scheduling, but it was not until the 1920s that real progress was made. The recently created Ancient Monuments Department of the Office of Works was actively encouraging owners to put their sites into guardianship while seeking, through local voluntary correspondents, for sites to schedule. Nationally nearly 3,000 sites were added to the new schedule of monuments between 1923 and 1931.[42] In 1921 the Roman site of Burgh Castle was scheduled, but the main burst of activity came in 1924/25, when the excursion secretary of the Norfolk Archaeological Society, Basil Cozens-Hardy, was responsible for submitting 190 sites to the Ancient Monuments Board. While the earliest monuments to be scheduled were medieval castles and abbeys, Cozens-Hardy identified a wide range of sites. These included Caistor Roman town and prehistoric remains such as Warham Iron Age camp. The Neolithic flint mines at Grimes Graves, whose significance had been understood following the excavations of the Rev. William Greenwell there in 1869-71, were of obvious importance. In 1917 Reginald Smith of the British Museum had requested that the monument be scheduled as it was 'incontestably the finest Stone Age site in England and probably elsewhere'. However, when the Forestry Commission (as a government department) bought the whole area in 1926, the scheduling became void and a large part of the area was planted with trees, the Commission claiming that its brief was to make the area as profitable as possible. However, the Office of Works countered by saying that the state must set an example in the management of historic sites. There was criticism in the press and after much negotiation the site was bought by the Office of Works in 1931.[43] Also scheduled were earthworks such as barrows and the Dark Age Devil's Dyke at Ashill (1924), the medieval ecclesiastical sites of Binham Priory and the cathedral site and bishop's chapel at North Elmham (1924), with Creake Abbey following in 1928. Early site descriptions, however, were sketchy and their extents seldom defined. Caister Castle, for instance, was described simply as a 'picturesque ruin'. In all 188 sites were protected by 1925, ensuring that, after Wiltshire, Norfolk had more Scheduled Ancient Monuments than any other county.[44] A further Ancient Monuments Act of 1931 introduced two new powers. Three months' notice had to be given before a scheduled

33  Burgh Castle was taken into Guardianship in 1921. The photograph shows
the state of the Roman walls before conservation work began.

34  Burgh Castle Roman Saxon-shore fort, as it is now, beside Breydon Water
(a Special Protection Area for birds and added to the Ramsar list of 'wetlands of
international importance' in 1996). The reed beds below the fort are an SSSI.
The Halvergate marshes can be seen on the other side of Breydon Water.
The fort and surrounding land is now owned and managed by the Norfolk
Archaeological Trust.

monument could be disturbed and the Crown was able to prosecute a person
for damaging a monument. The Act also protected the setting of a monument.
By 1950 about forty more sites had been added to the list. These included such
important sites as Brancaster Roman Fort, the abbeys at Coxford and Marham
and several ruined churches.[45] Almost 200 files in the National Archives (WORKS
14) contain correspondence from the 1920s and 1930s covering Norfolk sites to
be scheduled and brought into guardianship, as well as advice to owners on
conservation and repair.

Although the Ministry of Works has been empowered since 1883 to take monuments into guardianship, no sites in Norfolk were included until the 1920s.
Guardianship allowed the Ministry to take charge of monuments, whether or

not it owned them, and to open them to the public. One of the first was Castle Acre Priory, which was taken over from the Holkham estate in 1929; it was followed by Binham Priory in 1932. The site of the Saxon cathedral and ruins of the bishop's chapel at North Elmham, which had been cleared by the Victorian rector Augustus Legge, was not taken into guardianship until 1948, by which time it was heavily overgrown. The thickets were cleared, but there was no modern excavation until 1954 and 1958.[46] The Ancient Monuments Act of 1931 provided for the preparation of Presentation Schemes and restricted 'development within the vicinity of an Ancient Monument to ensure its preservation'. As with early scheduling, it was castles and abbeys which were most favoured. The iconic site of St Benet's Abbey in the Broads was offered by the Ecclesiastical Commissioners

*35 The iconic St Benet's Abbey was scheduled in 1915, soon after the passing of the Ancient Monuments Act in 1913. It has recently been conserved by the Norfolk Archaeological Trust with funding from the HLF and other charitable bodies.*

to the Ministry of Works three times between 1937 and 1954, but was refused each time, the first time because it was said to be in good repair and too isolated to attract visitors. In 1939 it was the cost of excavation which put the Ministry off, while no specific reason was given in 1954.[47] It has since been taken on by the NAT.

A later Chief Inspector of Ancient Monuments wrote that he saw the 1920s and 1930s as a 'golden age' in which the reputation of the Ministry and the management of its guardianship monuments was high.[48] Nearly all of the sixteen guardianship sites outside the main urban centres in Norfolk were taken on in this period – a time in which, according to Simon Thurley, the political interest

in national identity was high.[49] After the horrors of the First World War and the economic depression that followed there was a desire to connect people in an immediate and visible way with the achievements of the national story. The public were given the maximum degree of access and, from 1917, guide books began to be produced. By 1937 seventy-six sites nationally had guide books which often contained the first measured survey of the site to be made. While the technical nature of these drawings, showing different phases of construction and giving rather dry, detailed descriptions, do not contain the social context which makes a modern guide book more readable, they do represent an important step in the interpretation of ancient monuments and are a model of their type. As a rapidly increasing and varied range of mainly medieval ruins and building was taken on, a well-structured team of technically experienced foreman, superintendents, craftsmen and labourers were employed. Monuments and their surroundings were well cared for 'to a high, if perhaps over-trim degree'.[50] However, interwar ancient monument legislation was limited to the protection of individual sites and monuments; it did not cover areas, or buildings in use. This had to wait for the introduction of planning legislation.

## The Second World War

The war itself created problems for the Trusts, with much land in Norfolk being taken for airfields. Emergency excavations took place at Hethel in 1941 in advance of the airfield there.li The war effort itself sapped energy away from conservation. In 1944 there were even discussions on combining the NNNS and the NNT. However, Basil Cozens-Hardy repeated the view that he had held when the Trust was founded that such an arrangement would not be practical, as the Society was primarily academic and scientific while the Trust was a property-owning body incorporated for the purpose of owning land.[52]

We can see, therefore, how the major forces for conservation which were to grow in importance after 1945 originated in the interwar period: the two Norfolk-wide Trusts (NNT and NAT), the CPRE county branch, the increasing presence of the National Trust in the county, the launching of the Country House Scheme and the beginnings of the involvement of both local and national government were all in place by 1939. However, the main aim at this time was the preservation of important sites and habitats rather than a regard for the wider landscape. Membership, particularly of the NAT, was very small and there was no interest in opening to the public. While the National Trust had always welcomed visitors, who would be taken out in organised trips to walk through the tern colonies under the eye of the watcher,[53] the main concern for the NNT was protecting areas from too much disturbance. Opening up sites and interpreting historic places for the public was well understood by the Office of Works on their guardianship sites, but as far as natural habitats were concerned the conflicting aims of preservation and encouraging visitors remained unresolved.

1   Bull 1999, 40.
2   Sheail 1998, 6.
3   NRO C/C/10/19, 476 (April 1919).
4   *Eastern Daily Press* 15 November 1926.
5   Gay 1944.
6   H. Batsford (1940) 'Introduction' to *How To See The Country*. London, Batsford.
7   George 1992, 361-6.
8   T. Williamson (1997) *The Norfolk Broads: a landscape history*. Manchester, Manchester University Press, 159.
9   Ward Lock & Co. (n.d.) *The Broads*. London, 17.
10  Dutt 1905, 151.
11  TNA WORKS 14/1735.
12  *East Anglian Daily Times*, 3 January 1920.
13  *Eastern Daily Press*, 31 August 1935, 12.
14  G.C. Davies (1884) *Norfolk broads and rivers*, 2nd edn. Edinburgh and London, W. Blackwood and Son, 114.
15  Wade Martins and Williamson 2008, 91-100.
16  Dymond 1985, 250.
17  W.G. Clarke (1925) *In Breckland wilds*, Cambridge, Heffers, 31.
18  Holkham MS H/invB1.
19  M. Waterson (1994) *The National Trust: the first hundred years*. London, BBC/National Trust, 61.
20  For a biography of Lord Lothian see J.R.M. Butler (1960) *Lord Lothian*. Oxford, Oxford University Press.
21  Butler 1960, 145.
22  Waterson 2011, 41-50.
23  Information from Matthew Martins, formerly a partner in Cozons-Hardy and Jewson.
24  O.G.S. Crawford (1929) 'Editorial', *Antiquity* 3:2, quoted in Hunter 1996, 48.
25  Saunders 1983, 20.
26  The work of the early years of the NAT has been summarised from NRO uncat. Minute books of the Norfolk Archaeological Trust.
27  For details of Dr Long's life see Fowler 1976, 'Introduction'.
28  Sydney Long's scrap books in the archives of the NWT.
29  Minute books in the archives of the NWT.
30  Minute books in the archives of the NWT.
31  NNT minute book annual report 1949.
32  M. Kirby (1999) 'Nature' , in T. Heaton (ed.), *Norfolk century*. Norwich, *Eastern Daily Press*, 37.
33  Wade-Martins 1999, 311-12.
34  Sheail 1976, 61.
35  Sheail 2002, 126.
36  F.W. Oliver (1926-27) 'Nature reserves', TNNNS 12:3, 311-18.

37  CPRE Norwich office, uncatalogued archives.

38  E.W. Young (1996) Sixty years of the Norfolk Society. Norwich, Norfolk Society, 1-5

39  Letter by D.M.Matheson, secretary of the National Trust, to the *Eastern Daily Press*, March 2nd 1937.

40  E.W.Young 1996, 1-12.

41  George 1992, 401-6.

42  Hunter (ed) 1996, 48.

43  Thurley 2013, 101-6.

44  B.Cozens-Hardy 1926 'Scheduling of the Norfolk Ancient Monuments' *Norfolk Archaeology* 22 , 221-227.

45  *Development Plan for the County of Norfolk* 1951 NRO Acc 2012/163

46  S.E.Rigold 1961-3 'The Anglian cathedral of North Elmham, Norfolk' *Medieval Archaeology* 1-7, 51-66.

47  TNA WORKS 14/1735.

48  Saunders 1983, 19.

49  Thurley 2013, 256.

50  Saunders 1983, 20.

51  TNA WORK 14/1225.

52  NNT minute book. 1944.

53  Pers.com. John Sizer, National Trust.

# 4

## Brave New World – the immediate post-war years

Casual observers will see few drastic changes in the appearance of our fields in the near future. The patchwork quilt of colours and the different types and breeds of livestock will continue. (Gerald Wibberley 1950)[1]

### National policy and national parks

The view that the countryside was worth preserving had been gaining ground before the war, but had made little headway during the economic depression of the 1930s. But already in the darkest days of the Second World War there were those who were looking ahead to a better future. 'While almost everyone was busy with the immediate task of winning the war, it was also a time to dream of "a *forward looking* and bigger thing" than simply reverting to the pre-war days.'[2]

In 1941 the Scott Committee was formed to look ahead to what the British countryside should be like when peace returned. The committee, headed by Leslie Scott, a Lord Justice of Appeal, founder member of the CPRE and an active member of the Town and Country Planning Association, was set up to 'consider the conditions which should govern building and other constructional development in country areas consistent with the maintenance of agriculture ... having regard to ... the well-being of rural communities and the preservation of rural amenities'. The vice-chairman was Dudley Stamp, well respected for his work on the Land-use Survey and a member of the small group which established the agenda for the development of post-war rural planning policy.[3] His work had shown that between 1927 and 1939 there had been an average annual loss of 25,000 hectares of open land to urban and industrial development.[4] Scott, with his conservationist background, emphasised the aesthetic values of the countryside: 'The landscape of England and Wales is a striking example of the interdependence between the satisfaction of man's material wants and the creation of beauty', and so 'farmers and foresters are unconsciously the nation's landscape gardeners'.[5] He brought together the aspirations of the economist and the conservationist in the statement:

> We consider that the land of Britain should be both useful and beautiful and that the two aims are not incompatible. The only way to preserve the countryside in anything like its traditional aspect is to farm it.[6]

Scott and the majority of his committee thought it was traditional farming that would conserve the beauty and diversity of the countryside. Indeed, the eminent ecologist Arthur Tansley wrote in 1945: 'It is scarcely possible that the extension of agriculture will go much further; the limits of profitable agricultural land must have been reached in most places.'[7] However, the Scott Committee was not unanimous in its views. A minority report by Lord Dennison foresaw the dangers to the environment of an increasingly large-scale and automated agriculture.

Alongside these visions of the future of the countryside as a whole there was pressure for the development of national parks as a way of protecting some of the most valuable landscapes. This had begun with the Addison Committee report of 1931 and continued under the Standing Committee of National Parks, set up in 1936. In 1938 the Standing Committee published *The case for National Parks in Britain* and its ideas were taken up by Scott. His report, published in 1942, advocated tighter planning rules, the setting up of national parks, which would include both the Norfolk Broads and the entire coastline of England and Wales as a single national park, the establishment of a 'footpaths commission' and the registration of common land. In the same year John Dower was asked to undertake a survey of potential national parks and 'amenity areas'. The aims of the national parks would be to preserve their characteristic landscapes, to provide access for public open-air enjoyment, to protect wildlife, buildings and places of architectural and historical interest, and to ensure that established farming use was effectively maintained. 'It was the culmination of inter-war attempts to combine preservation with modernity.'[8] In a lecture to the RIBA in 1943 John Dower explained why he thought that national parks would be so important. The holiday use of the countryside would be a significant part of post-war reconstruction, contributing to the physical and mental health of the nation. There would be increased leisure time and an increasing popular appreciation of 'natural landscape beauty', and all this would be made possible by the advance of mechanical transport.[9]

The official view was thus seen to support conservation and so be in tune with the national park movement. However, the problem remained over the conflict between access, recreation and conservation. There needed to be a clear difference between national parks and national nature reserves (NNRs). The protection of 'natural beauty' was the role of national parks, while nature reserves were for the protection of nature. In June 1941 (the same year as the Scott Committee was set up) a 'conference on nature preservation in post-war reconstruction' was organised by the Society for the Promotion of Nature Reserves (SPNR) and the RSPB. In 1942 a Nature Reserve Investigation Committee was created under Arthur Tansley and regional sub-committees were formed. The importance of the designation of NNRs based on scientific evidence was stressed. The sub-committee for Norfolk included many well-known naturalists and was chaired by Anthony Buxton of the Horsey Estate in Norfolk. It reported in August 1943 and recommended that all the Broadland rivers and their assoc iated broads, marshes and tributaries should be 'scheduled areas'. Three areas, Hickling–Horsey, Ranworth–Woodbastwick and Wheatfen, should be given priority rating.[10] There are now at least twenty NNRs in Norfolk concentrated in the Broads, the heaths of Breckland, west Norfolk and the north coast.

At the same time, a final list of ten areas that should be designated national parks was being recommended in the Dower Report of 1945. which included the Broads as a 'reserve area.' Owing to disagreement between the government departments involved, the Dower report was not endorsed and instead a National Parks Committee (the Hobhouse Committee), working in parallel with a Wildlife and Conservation Committee chaired by Julian Huxley, was set up to review John Dower's report and the different approaches needed to nature conservation and national parks. The Hobhouse Report of 1947 included the Broads in a third instalment list of national parks to be established. It described the area as

> a unique complex of fens and waterways which provides unsurpassed opportunities for sailing and boating holidays, a distinctive range of flora and fauna, including many rare and interesting specimens, and a delicate beauty of landscape, derived from the integration of water and land, and the soft colourings of the marshlands under a wide sky. It will be the only National Park in the eastern counties; and has the added advantage of being easily accessible from London and the Midlands.[11]

However, in spite of this glowing assessment the Broads remained on a reserve list. This was because

> there are many complications, both of drainage, navigation etc., and of existing misuses and disfigurements; and the requirements differ materially from those of a regular National Park. It may prove better to deal with the area on some ad hoc scheme of combined local and national action, which should include the protection of substantial areas of mere and marsh as strict Nature Reserves.[12]

There was also the problem of costs. The committee estimated these over a ten-year programme for the rehabilitation of the region, including clearing vegetation, dredging channels, providing mooring facilities and wardening, as £122,100 in the first year and £117,000 in each of the following nine. This greatly reduced its chances of gaining national park status.[13] Not surprisingly, therefore, the Broads were not included in the National Parks Act of 1949.

Meanwhile, in 1947 the Huxley Committee recommended nearly 100 NNRs across Britain. These were on a much smaller scale than the large areas in national parks and were chosen for their wildlife, ecological or geological importance. Norfolk examples included Scolt Head and Blakeney Point on the north coast, and Hickling Broad, Horsey Mere, Barton Broad and Winterton Dunes in the Broads and on the east coast. In Breckland, Cavenham Heath, Lakenheath and Wangford Warren, all of which 'displayed a set of conditions and communities found nowhere else in these islands' were included.[14] Parts of Wangford

Common and Lakenheath were already protected, as they were owned by the NNT. However, there were many sites which could not be recommended as NNRs, mainly because they were smaller and important for very specific reasons. To draw attention to their importance the Committee suggested that they should be scheduled separately as Sites of Special Scientific Interest (SSSIs). It also encouraged the designation of Local Nature Reserves. As early as 1929 Professor Oliver had seen local groups such as the NNT as the ideal bodies to manage them and by 1946 the NNT had acquired seven reserves divided between the north Norfolk coast, the Broads and Breckland.

In 1944 Major Buxton proposed a Broadland Nature Reserve. His family had established a bird sanctuary at Horsey in 1910 which was world famous as a breeding ground for wildfowl.[15] He felt that the property should be owned by the National Trust, with the NNT cooperating in its management. The NNT committee agreed that the site should go to the National Trust 'and in any case no further steps should be taken until the government's actions as regards nature reserves in general was made known'.[16]

Nearly all the pressure at this time was focused on the natural environment, with little official interest shown in the protection of the cultural landscape. 'Though the Ministry of Works has fairly wide powers, we are not satisfied that the conjoined interests are sufficiently met.' The Huxley Committee recognised this as a serious omission, stating in its report:

> We are neither directed nor qualified to consider archaeological values; but, as we have tried to show, the interests with which we are concerned are closely involved, and we should like to see applied to archaeological principles of preservation and conservation similar to those we are seeking to apply in our own sciences. We therefore strongly recommend that a special committee fully competent to advise on these aspects should be set up without delay; and meanwhile, that in any proposed legislation, provision should be made to include archaeological features in the general conservation and planning machinery.[17]

No such committee was set up and the conservation of field monuments lagged well behind that of wildlife.

One of the tasks of the Nature Conservancy, set up under the National Parks Act of 1949, was to designate SSSIs and NNRs. The Breckland Heaths, the Broads as a whole and the north Norfolk coast were all considered areas of scientific interest. Professor Steers had been studying Scolt Head since the 1920s and was instrumental in its becoming one of the first Norfolk National Nature Reserves in 1954. For many years, until his death in 1987, he was chairman of both the Scolt Head Joint Advisory Committee and the Norfolk Coast Conservation Committee. He understood that coastal conservation needed the support of the local population, particularly those who made their living from the sea. He had a gentle but firm authority which commanded respect, was an enthusiastic supporter of all research at Scolt Head and understood the importance of earth and life sciences working together to protect the coastline.[18]

Government concern over the conservation of the Broads can be traced back to 1944, when the Minister of Town and Country Planning wrote to Norfolk County Council indicating that 'the time is ripe for an investigation into problems connected with the preservation, control and improvement' of Broadland and requesting the organising of a Broads conference of interested parties. This was held in April 1945 and resulted in the production of a list of eight factors which were detracting from the beauty of the Broads. These including pollution and rubbish, the increase in river traffic, the 'erection of bungalows and shacks', the contraction of the area of open water by weed growth and the decay of old pumping mills and other traditional buildings.[19] A further conference was held in 1947 which recommended the setting up of a Broads Committee as a voluntary body 'to promote the welfare, development and use' of the Broads. It would be a consultative body, advising and stimulating existing authorities to exercise their powers by negotiating between opposing interests and making recommendations.[20] In 1949 a Broads Joint Advisory Committee was set up with the function of advising the planning authorities with responsibility in the area. However, it was primarily concerned with development control and planning and did not attempt to tackle the environmental problems that were building up.

The immediate post-war years were active ones for the NNT. In 1945 it was asked by the Huxley Committee to produce a map 'showing all areas which they regarded as important for the conservation of flora and fauna, together with a note stating in reference to each area what particular danger (development, forestry, change in landuse) they thought should be guarded against'.[21] A copy of this map could not be located.

36 *Dr Joyce Lambert at work in the Norfolk Broads. Her pioneering botanical research, alongside the historical and geological evidence, established that the Broads were man-made medieval peat diggings.*

Building on its previous success, the NNT turned its attention to the Broads, which were likely to come under increased pressure as peace allowed the holiday industry to expand. In 1945 part of Barton Broad was given to the NNT by Captain Wilson of Irstead Lodge, while the northern part was purchased from a Mr Storey, and in the same year the Whiteslea estate at the south end of Hickling Broad was purchased from Lord Desborough's executors with the help of Christopher Cadbury, the RSPB, the Pilgrim Trust and a national appeal. An endowment fund of £15,000 to support the reserve was needed and a national appeal was over-subscribed by £2,360.[22] Meanwhile, Major Buxton sold his property at Horsey to the National Trust for £5,000. The area became immediately popular and 'The difficulties arising from the large numbers of visitors to Hickling Broad' were discussed by the NNT committee; 'it was resolved that in future these should be limited to subscribers of a minimum of one pound. Permission must be obtained from the secretary.'[23] In 1948 forty acres in the Yare Valley at Surlingham were given to the Trust and the following year Ranworth and the smaller Cockshoot Broad, off the River Bure, were given by Colonel Cator subject to the king having one day of shooting a year. No visitors were to be allowed into these areas except to the watchtower at the end of the Broad, 'from which there is an excellent view'.[24] However, an appeal for the upkeep of these two Broads was far less successful than the earlier one and the fact that there was far less public interest in maintenance than in purchase had to be accepted. In 1952 Surlingham Broad was purchased with the help of £1,000 from the Pilgrim Trust. By this time the NNT holdings in the Broads were substantial and a sub-committee to manage them was set up. The NNT annual report of 1950 reported that

> Naturalists from all over the country and overseas visited the Norfolk Nature Reserves, particularly those established in the Broads and on the coast.
> The number of visitors increased every year and many expressed appreciation of the facilities provided by the Trust and 'the help so courteously given by the wardens.

Outside these protected areas progress in the Broads was painfully slow, as naturalists and scientists watched an area once famed for its flora and fauna being reduced to mediocrity. There were too many competing interests — tourism, farming, drainage and other local authorities — for a unified approach to be achieved. In 1952 new research led by the Norfolk-born botanist Dr Joyce Lambert showed that the Broads were of interest not only to the naturalist but also to the historian. She announced her findings in her presidential address to the NNNS. By analysing more than 1,500 borings from the deposits of peats, clays and muds she was able to show that the broads had had vertical sides and flat bottoms criss-crossed by steep-sided ridges and islands of solid peat, often associated with parish boundaries. The only logical explanation was that they were not in fact natural lakes, but man-made peat diggings dating back to the Middle Ages. Her findings then found support from work by Dr Clifford Smith on medieval leases, surveys and other documents.[25]

Meanwhile, the pollution of the Broads continued to give concern. As early as 1921 boating interests were complaining that Hickling Broad was becoming choked with weed which would spoil the annual regatta, as well as the fishing.

A letter to the *Eastern Daily Press* suggested that clearing the weed would be 'useful work for the unemployed'.[26] The seriousness of the problems were highlighted in a report of the Nature Conservancy in 1965, followed in 1971 by publication of Norfolk County Council's first *Broadland Study and Plan*. But little action followed and it was the floating of a proposal for a national park in the late 1970s that resulted in pressure on all the county authorities to come up with a joint programme of proper management to halt, and if possible reverse, the decline. While the Countryside Commission and the conservation bodies saw a national park status as the only possible solution the various local authorities and recreational interests feared just another layer of bureaucracy and in January 1978, after a 'long and complex debate', the Norfolk County Council voted against supporting a national park, a decision criticised by the *Eastern Daily Press* in its leader: 'The only common ground is that something must be done quickly if the Broads are to be saved, but the most likely effect of the County Council's deplorable decision is that effective action, of whatever nature and from within whatever framework, will be further delayed.'[27] The compromise was the setting-up, after long negotiation, of a joint Broads Authority consisting of representatives of the eight local authorities, the Countryside Commission, Anglian Water and the Great Yarmouth Port and Haven Commissioners. According to the Agreement signed in 1980, the Authority would be funded from the local authorities and operate from offices provided by Broadland District in Norwich. The planning functions of the participating local authorities within the Broads were to be devolved to the Authority and one of the main tasks was to produce a new management plan for the region. A consultative document, 'What future for Broadland', was produced in 1982 and a final lavishly illustrated 128-page version, the *Broads Plan*, in 1987.[28] There always had to be compromises. As stated in the original Agreement, consideration of the wildlife importance of the region had to be balanced against the 'economic and social interests of those who live and work in the area (and) ... facilitating the use of the Broads for holiday and recreational purposes'. Finally, in 1988, fifty-eight years after the Addison Committee had recommended that the Broads should be a national park, legislation giving the Broads Authority National Park status in all but one important aspect was passed. To placate the boating and tourism interests, the bill for its creation, unlike that of other national parks, did not include the stipulation that 'if an

*37 The Ouse Washes, acquired by the Wildlife and Wetlands Trust in 1971, are an important feeding ground for migrating wetland birds.*

irreconcilable conflict of interest occurs within a national park, priority should be given to the conservation of natural beauty' over economic arguments (the Sandford principle).[29] In effect, the Broads Act 1988 requires balanced weight to be given to navigation as against conservation.

From its inception, the Authority supported a wide range of academic research studying the nutrient levels in the sediments deposited in the Broads and why their ecology had changed so profoundly since 1945. The water chemistry and the way in which water plants were affected by increasing nutrient levels was also a subject for scientific investigation. In this the Authority was greatly assisted by work undertaken by Brian Moss and his colleagues in the School of Environmental Sciences, set up as part of the new University of East Anglia when it opened its doors in 1963.

The NNT's progress in Breckland was not so impressive. The purchase of 225 acres on Thetford Heath was followed by the news that Stanford Battle Area was to be extended to include much of the Wretham reserve, and in 1953

> The proposal to develop Thetford and Brandon into towns capable of absorbing 300,000 Londoners for work in the timber industry was considered a possible threat to the Trust's reserves. It was agreed that the government department responsible for National Parks and NNRs, the Nature Conservancy (later English Nature)should be consulted.[30]

The restriction on the number of members of the NNT seems to have been dropped after the war; there were 321 life members by 1947, when membership cards were introduced, and 760 by 1951, many of whom were annual subscribers. For the first time a leaflet listing the properties owned by the Trust was produced for members. Further efforts to involve members were made in 1955, when the AGM was to be made more attractive by the inclusion of a film or lecture. In 1960 it was resolved that 'an effort be made to encourage more activity on the part of Trust members and the possibility of arranging excursions in future years'. Notice boards were installed at Hickling Broad and on Breckland.[31]

A further area of great ornithological importance is the Wash. It is one of Britain's most important winter feeding areas for waders and wildfowl outside the breeding season. The RSPB took over the marshes at Snettisham, visited by thousands of migrating waders every year, in 1972. Peter Scott lived in the Nene Lighthouse at the north-west edge of the county for many years. The reserve on the important marshland feeding grounds of the Ouse Washes at Welney was set up in 1971 by the Wildlife and Wetlands Trust, which was founded by Sir Peter Scott at Slimbridge (Gloucestershire) in 1946. The Welney reserve consists of over 1,000 acres of seasonally flooded land, making it the largest such site in Britain.The whole coastline of tidal mudflats and sands from the Nene around the Wash to Snettisham was leased to the Nature Conservancy and is protected by them.

## The historic environment and planning for the future

While concern for the natural environment was growing, the immediate post-war years saw the wholesale demolition of country houses. The agricultural depression and accompanying falls in rents had meant that many landed gentry had abandoned their great houses in the 1920s and 1930s, and they stood unwanted and in disrepair, an ever-increasing burden on ever-decreasing fortunes. Some were taken over by the military during the Second World War and so had suffered further degradation. Following the war the armies of servants and estate staff that were needed to run them were no longer available and only the finest examples, where the owner could provide an endowment to support them, could be taken over by the National Trust. The result was the destruction of many. In Norfolk fifty-four disappeared in the twentieth century, 40 per cent between 1940 and 1960.[32] The loss of the house usually meant the end of the parkland around it and the combination meant a diminution of the cultural and landscape diversity of the locality. The scale of the loss was brought home by an exhibition at the Victoria and Albert Museum in the winter of 1974 entitled *The Destruction of the Country House*. As publicity for the exhibition, photographs of lost houses were sent to local newspapers and public awareness was raised. The result was the founding of SAVE in 1975, whose aim was to publicise threats to historic buildings.

The deaths of the third earl of Leicester in 1941, followed only eight years later by that of the fourth earl, left Holkham very vulnerable to death duties and overtures were made to the National Trust. Lord Crawford, chairman of the National Trust, described the hall as being 'the noblest and the library the cosiest room in England' and wrote to the fifth earl, 'I can from my own experience realise the sort of dilemma you are in and the sense of hopelessness and helplessness one feels.'[33] In the event some of the outlying farms were sold, as well as books and manuscripts from the library, which government grants enabled the British Museum and the Bodleian Library to buy. In 1950 the house was opened for nine afternoons in July and August, bringing in just over £1,000, a figure that doubled the next year. An important milestone for Holkham and other privately owned houses was the publication of the Gowers report and the implementation of its recommendations in 1953. This established the Historic Buildings Council, which

38  *Burnham Overy Mill — an example of one of the 'Amenity Areas' recognised in the* 1951 County Development Plan.

had the power to award grants for the maintenance of buildings, and the Ministry of Works architect gave enthusiastic support to Holkham, which benefited greatly from these grants from their inception.[34]

The period also saw an increasing involvement of local government in planning and preservation. As we have seen, the CPRE was critical of the lack of effective planning controls in the 1930s, despite the planning acts of 1923, 1932 and 1935. As with the moves towards national parks, concerns over planning for a better future also began in the later years of the Second World War, when the need for control over rebuilding after the war became clear. The real change was the Town and Country Planning Act of 1947, which gave control of planning to the new Local Planning Authorities (LPAs). For rural Norfolk the LPA was Norfolk County Council, which excluded the County Boroughs of Norwich and Great Yarmouth. The LPA was required to produce a County Development Plan which would guide planning decisions for the next twenty years, and the *Plan* for Norfolk was published in 1951. For the first time the concept of identifying areas of 'high landscape value' was recognised and the plan contained sections on 'National Parks, Conservation and Amenity Considerations' and 'Ancient Monuments and Buildings of Architectural and Historic Interest'. As well as nationally recognised sites, the Plan identified for the first time 'Amenity Areas' such as Blickling, Burnham Overy Mill and Roman Camp, West Runton. The Broads and the north Norfolk coast were recognised as being of 'Landscape Value'. In 1968 the north Norfolk coast was designated an Area of Outstanding Natural Beauty (AONB). The need for conservation was not only seen to include specific ring-fenced recognised sites but also flagged up the need for some control over much larger areas. The implementation of the plan was left largely to local Urban and Rural District Councils, with professional planning advice from the county planning department and with the proviso that any proposal contrary to the *Plan* should be referred to the County Council.

While there had been considerable pressure on government to create national parks and nature reserves, there had been little concern over historic sites. The construction of motorways, road widening schemes and city bypasses were the first linear threat since the the construction of the railways. Gravel workings associated with these new roads proliferated, especially along river valleys rich in prehistoric settlement. Aerial photography was revealing ever more sites at a time when forestry and modern farming, with its deep ploughing and drainage schemes, were posing ever greater threats. 'Economic incentives offered by post-war agricultural incentives and tax structures turned agriculture into a serious threat to rural archaeology.'[35] The number of scheduled monuments in Norfolk had hardly risen since the 1920s, when Basil Cozens-Hardy had been active, but by 1950 sixty-four new sites were 'under consideration'. 'A number of the more important ones (already scheduled) are in direct custodianship of the Ministry of Works and are usually open to inspection on payment of a small fee.'[36] This number has risen to over 400.

Appreciation of the regional diversity of the built environment was also increasing. Attempts to identify buildings of historic and architectural interest other than those recognised as Ancient Monuments had begun in the last days of the Second World War. The 1947 Town and Country Planning Act gave local authorities or central government the power to make 'lists' of historic buildings, but there was no obligation to do so or any mechanism for regulating the destruction or alteration of such buildings. Archaeological considerations were given very little weight. In 1945 an advisory committee on listing was established to provide guidance on how the system should operate and it decided that there should be three grades. It then oversaw the first survey of the nation's historic buildings. Under the 1947 Act listing became a statutory duty of government, 'thus presaging the most comprehensive act of state intervention in heritage that had hitherto been seen'.[37] Provisional lists were compiled from 1948 by the Ministry of Works and included over 1,500 Norfolk buildings by 1951. Buildings were classified as grade I, II* and II, but until 1968 no particular statutory powers were attached to these classifications. In Norfolk, the future of windmills was a particular concern. By 1951 twenty-six had been listed; in contrast, water mills were not thought to be at such a risk, with only eleven included.[38] Only in 1966 was this national listing survey finally completed. Churches, country houses and vernacular buildings dating from before about 1800 made up the majority of buildings included. However, local authorities had very little power to prevent the alteration or demolition of listed buildings. The Historic Buildings and Ancient Monuments Act of 1953 set up the Historic Buildings Council, which could give grants to owners of listed properties. It also repealed the preservation order arrangements of 1913 and 1931 and introduced a revised system of 'Interim Preservation Notices' and 'Guardianship Orders'. In 1962 local authorities were given the power to make similar grants. The 1968 Town and Country Planning Act legislated that permission for grade I and II* was needed before demolition or alterations were undertaken and fines were in place for unauthorised works. Grants for repair could also be given. These early lists were indeed little more than that, with only the briefest of descriptions of the buildings concerned. This left room for revision and improvement, which was undertaken at a later date.

The post-war years saw a steady increase in standards of living and car ownership alongside increased leisure and a desire to visit and understand the countryside. The production of popular books, which had begun before the war, continued. Robert Hale, under the general editorship of Brian Vesey Fitzgerald, was producing a series of both regional (*The Broads* and *The Fens*, both 1952, and *Breckland* in 1956) and county (*Norfolk*, 1951) books. The Norfolk volume boasted on its cover 'the immense variety of scenery, fine examples of all that is best of English architecture, great variety of landscape and a rich historic past'. Separate sections covered the Broads, Breckland, the Fens and the coast. Particularly popular was Faber and Faber's series of 'Shell Guides', edited by John Betjeman and sponsored by the oil company. The authors of the Norfolk volume, published in 1957, claimed to have visited 'every church, village and country house within the county .... Everything Norfolk has to show that is worth mentioning is mentioned here.'[39] This popular interest increased awareness and pressure for the preservation of what were seen as significant monuments from the past, although these were generally confined to the churches, castles, ruined abbeys and great houses that featured so prominently in the guide books.

Concentration was still focused on individual sites and buildings rather than larger areas. Change had to await the 'Civic Amenities Act' (1967), which introduced the concept of 'Conservation Areas'. These were defined as 'Areas of Special Architectural or Historic interest, the character or appearance of which it is desirable to preserve or enhance'.[40]

Gradually the emphasis in the conservation of both natural and historic sites was shifting from single isolated examples to concern for the wider environment. This was a trend which increased during the later years of the twentieth century, but at the same time was likely to be more controversial. The conflicts which resulted are the subject of the next chapter.

1   Quoted in P. Lowe, C. Cox, M. MacEwen, T. O'Rioden and M. Winter (1986) *Countryside conflict: the politics of farming, forestry and conservation*. Aldershot, Gower, 26.
2   Sheail 2002, 117.
3   W. Pilfold (2007) 'Defending farmland', in B. Short, C. Watkins and J. Martin (ed.) *The Front Line of Freedom*. Exeter, British Agricultural History Society, 196.
4   Lowe et al. 1986, 16.
5   Scott, Lord Justice (1942) Report of the Committee of Land Utilisation in Rural Areas. Command Paper 6278, London, HMSO, 4.
6   Scott 1942, 47.
7   A. Tansley (1945) *Our heritage and wild nature: a plea for organised nature conservation*; quoted in Lowe et al. 1986, 20.

8   Sheail 2002, 121.

9   Sheail 2002, 118.

10  George 1992, 453.

11  Parliamentary Papers (1947) Report of the National Parks Committee (England and Wales) (the Hobhouse report). Command Paper 7121, London, HMSO, 11.

12  PP 1947 7121, quoted in George 1992, 408.

13  George 1992, 408.

14  Parliamentary Papers (1947) Report on the Conservation of Nature in England and Wales (the Huxley Report). Command Paper 7122, London, HMSO, 22.

15  *Eastern Daily Press*, 17 May 1946.

16  NNT minute book 1944.

17  TNA HLG 93/23; Parliamentary Papers 1947b, 32 and 30.

18  H. Allison and J. Morley (eds) (1989) *Blakeney Point and Scolt Head Island*. Norfolk, National Trust, 10.

19  Quoted in George 1992, 407.

20  Printed report of conference (NCC).

21  NNT Minute book 1945.

22  *Eastern Daily Press*, 17 May 1946.

23  NNT minute books 1946.

24  NNT minute books 1949.

25  J. Lambert, J. Jennings, C. Smith, C. Green and J. Hutchison (1960) *The Making of the Broads*. Royal Geographical Society, Series 3. London, RGS.

26  *Eastern Daily Press*, letter 21 November 1921.

27  *Eastern Daily Press*, 24 January 1978.

28  George 1992, 424-7.

29  George 1992, 438.

30  NNT minute books 1953.

31  NNT minute books 1947, 1951, 1955 and 1960.

32  D. Clarke (2008) *The country houses of Norfolk*, part two, the lost houses. Wymondham, George Reeve, 5.

33  Holkham MS 'sale of heirlooms file' correspondence 1949-1950.

34  I am grateful to Christine Hiskey, the archivist at Holkham, for the information in this paragraph.

35  Hunter 1996, 51.

36  Norfolk County Council (1951) *Development Plan for the County of Norfolk*. Norwich, NCC (NRO Acc2012/163). For an analysis of the 1951 report see J. Ayton (2012) 'The mid-twentieth century norfolk county survey and plan', *The Annual* 21, 15-32.

37  Cowell 2008, 112.

38  Norfolk County Council 1951; Ayton 2012.

39  W. Harrod and C.L.S. Linnell (1957) *Shell Guide to Norfolk*. London, Faber (dust cover).

40  Mynors 2006, 12-13.

# 5

# Conflict and compromise: into the twenty-first century

> The present generation is witnessing the most comprehensive and far-reaching changes of the natural history and historical landscape of Britain ever experienced in such a short period of time.[1]

From the 1960s the perception of what conservation in the countryside meant gradually changed. Sometimes described as the 'democratisation of the countryside', this has been to a great extent the result of an increasing awareness among the population in general, rather than just a minority of the professional and leisured classes, of the huge value of the natural and cultural heritage and of the varied landscape in which we live. Increased leisure time, along with the availability of transport, has all been part of this process. Gradually the word 'preservation', suggesting a static situation of ring-fenced specific historic sites or ecologically sensitive areas, was replaced by 'conservation', allowing for wider landscapes to be recognised and a realisation that by sensitive management different uses could co-exist.

While the early naturalists were concerned with the protection of particular species rather than their habitat, and the antiquarians with the finds from their excavations rather than the sites themselves, by the end of the nineteenth century these attitudes were beginning to change. Wildlife could only flourish if the environment was right, and the monuments as well as their contents were of value. From the 1950s these ideas were also expanded by an understanding that wildlife could often not survive within the tight boundaries of reserves: wider corridors linking these protected areas were also needed. In the same way, the setting of ancient monuments needed protecting if they were to be fully understood within their landscape.

Not only have our ideas of what conservation really means shifted over this period, but we can distinguish four elements in the development of the conservation movement, all of which are well illustrated by the conflicts and compromises in the Norfolk countryside. These four strands include nature and wildlife, rural landscape, archaeological remains and historic buildings. While these themes often overlap, the experience of Norfolk reveals differences in the level of public and political interest, in financial support from government, in the role of the voluntary sector, in the relevant institutional frameworks and in legislative powers.

## Nature and wildlife: agriculture and conservation

For the first time a clash between agriculture and conservation began to emerge, largely as a result of increased public awareness of the damage modern farming caused to wildlife and the visual landscape. The war-time Scott Committee had seen the existence of a well-farmed and prosperous landscape as the key to a vibrant and diverse countryside well managed for the benefit of man and nature. 'There is a community of interests between agriculture and amenity.' The threats, as Scott saw them, were from new building, mainly in the form of ribbon development, and poorly sited industry. The best way of protecting the countryside was to retain the existing area of farming and limit the encroachment of development into and within the countryside. Farmers were its best custodians.[ii] However, as the horse disappeared from farms in the 1950s, to be replaced by ever-more powerful diesel tractors which needed ever larger fields in which to operate, and chemicals came to play an even greater part in farming practice in the form of fertilisers, herbicides and insecticides, agriculture came to be seen more as a threat to, rather than a protector, of the countryside. Rachel Carson's book *Silent Spring*, published in 1963, highlighted the dangers of the well-known insecticide DDT (chlorinated hydrocarbon) entering the food chain of many birds and proved to be the moment when the dangers of modern farming to the environment hit home to the public. Science and technology, which had been so generously funded by business and government, became increasingly associated with pollution and the destruction of habitats and diversity. These points were again brought home in Nan Fairbrother's seminal book *New Lives, New Landscapes*, published in 1970. Howard Newby dates the moment at which farmers changed from being seen as protectors to enemies of the countryside to 1973 and a speech given by the urban planner Sir Colin Buchanan to the CPRE. He described farmers as 'the most ruthless section of the business community' and 'a real danger to the countryside'.[3]

At the same time as the ecological threats to the countryside were being recognised, the infant subject of landscape history was gaining recognition. W.G. Hoskins' trail-blazing book *The Making of the English Landscape*, published in 1955, influenced a whole generation of historians and archaeologists. It led to the recognition of the diverse and now fast-changing landscape and its buildings as a source of history. This was followed in 1986 by the botanist Oliver Rackham's *History of the Countryside*, which stressed the importance of trees and hedgerows to an understanding of the landscape.

As farming changed and employment in agriculture declined, the farming industry came in for more and more criticism. The destruction, often with the encouragement of government subsidies, of archaeological sites and natural habitats by the ploughing-up and drainage of old grasslands and the use of more powerful machinery, as well as the grubbing up of hedges, became an ever-greater threat. Between 1946 and 1981 58 per cent of Norfolk's hedgerows were removed. Fifty per cent of ancient, semi-natural woodland remaining in 1945 had gone by 1973, 73 per cent of the 1946 grassland had been ploughed up and only 7 per cent of the remaining was herb-rich unimproved land and heathland. Old pits, often dug in the nineteenth century for marl, were filled in, thus reducing the diversity of wildlife habitats.[4] Archaeological earthwork sites, too, were being bulldozed, deep-ploughed and sub-soiled. Once the statutory three-month advance notice for destruction of a scheduled site had been given no further permission was needed. The effects of more intensified farming were recognised by 1954, when the number of inspectors employed by the Ministry of Works was increased with the aim of scheduling more grassland sites. In 1968 the Walsh Committee was set up to review the importance of field monuments on amenity and archaeological grounds alongside a government enquiry into the effects of plough damage on archaeological monuments. As a result of their findings local authorities were urged to do more to protect their monuments. This resulted in a Field Monuments Act of 1972, which introduced the concept of Acknowledgement Payments to farmers, who agreed to keep monuments out of cultivation. However, the payments were too small to be effective. By the mid 1970s it was recognised that earthwork sites were disappearing rapidly and that the level of the Acknowledgement Payment provided no incentive to protect them. The annual payment was £35, while the loss of income from not ploughing was nearer £95. When the barrows of Norfolk were surveyed in the 1930s almost all were in good condition, while in the 1970s fifty-three of the 162 scheduled barrows were being ploughed and only thirteen were more than fifty cms high.[5] An important change came with the 1979 Ancient Monuments and Archaeological Areas Act, which required landowners to apply for formal consent (rather than just give notice) before undertaking any works that would affect a Scheduled Ancient Monument. If the land was already ploughed this included any work liable to disturb the soil below the maximum depth affected by normal ploughing. The Acknowledgement Payment scheme was ended and instead, under Section 17 of the Act, English Heritage could make grants to farmers and landowners for good conservation management of scheduled and other monuments of schedulable quality, including taking sites out of arable use.

It was not only farming that was seen as a threat. Michael Dower's *The fourth wave: the challenge of leisure* (1965) listed the events over the previous 200 years which had challenged the environment. First was the Industrial Revolution and its coal-fired factories in mushrooming industrial towns, and then there were the railways. Thirdly, there were car-based suburbs and finally, in the second half of the twentieth century, there was an increasing demand for outdoor recreation. A desire to enjoy open spaces and natural scenery which could now be satisfied by a far larger proportion of the population than previously was in danger of destroying the very sources of that pleasure. In the Norfolk Broads, for example, the first comprehensive plan for the area identified two principal

*39 The Broads Wildlife Centre at Ranworth was opened by the Norfolk Wildlife Trust in 1976. This floating centre provides an opportunity for the interpretation of the whole Broads area.*

*40 The silent and environmentally friendly Broads Authority 'electric eel',
moored at How Hill and ready to take groups out.*

problems: the conflict between the expansion of holiday and recreational activities and the natural character of Broadland; and the conflicting demands of the
various recreational uses for a limited amount of water space.[6]

From the mid-1960s Norfolk experienced a rapid increase in the rate of population growth. This reflected expansion of employment in the towns, retirement migration, mainly from the south-east, and London overspill schemes
in Kings Lynn and Thetford under the Town Development Act of 1952. During
the 1970s and 1980s this acceleration in the county's overall population was
associated with a dispersal of new housing into the countryside. Despite county
planning policies that aimed to focus much new development into selected
settlements, the result of such pressures has been to 'suburbanise' the character

of many expanded villages as well as the fringes of market towns.[7] The impact of widespread housing estates and smaller-scale infill development in villages, together with the growth of tourism and the intensification of farming, were threats very much at the heart of the challenges facing conservationists in Norfolk.

Attitudes to visitors changed dramatically from the 1960s. The inter-war period had seen the development of a general suspicion of the 'uneducated' urban working class and their approach to the countryside. These were the people who broke fences, left litter and gates open, picked wild flowers rather than admiring them in their natural habitat, frightened birds and scrawled graffiti on historic buildings.[8] This attitude is clearly illustrated in the case of Wretham Heath, 368 acres of which had been owned by the NNT since 1938. The rapid expansion of nearby Thetford to accommodate London overspill was seen by some as a threat to the undisturbed nature of this Breckland reserve. Dogwalkers from neighbouring Attleborough wrote letters to the Eastern Daily Press complaining about ex-Londoners who left litter. Ted Ellis, in his weekly article 'In the Countryside' of 22 May 1970, wrote that Wretham Heath should be treated as 'a priceless heritage rather than a mere open space for every kind of frolic'. It was a nature reserve designed for people who wanted to learn more about nature and to do so in peace.[9] The problem was how to manage such sites for public enjoyment while at the same time ensuring nature conservation, educational use and scientific study. The NNT's solution in the case of Wretham was the creation of a Nature Trail guiding the public, with the help of a leaflet, on a marked route through the various landscapes of Breckland, thus leaving areas of the reserve undisturbed. That the NNT were able successfully to balance these needs was indicated by the support the Trust received from the public, as shown by its membership figures. While growing steadily in the 1950s to 900, in 1962 numbers suddenly shot up to 4,104 by 1972 and to 7,170 over the next decade, reaching 35,000 by 2012.

The 1960s saw similar conservation and educational work on the Broadland reserves. Up until then, apart from Hickling, where the head keeper would, by appointment, take up to four birdwatchers on a conducted tour, no reserve provided any guidance to either ornithologists or less specialist visitors. From 1963 a wide range of facilities began to be developed at Hickling by the NNT. Shallow lagoons and scrapes to attract waterfowl were created and new and larger hides built. In 1968 a thatched observation room was built and used as a base for the various self-guided walks and in 1970 a water-trail allowing visitors to see the banks of the broad from a boat was introduced. By the 1980s Hickling was attracting over 2,000 visitors a year. But the NNT wanted not only to introduce visitors to the delights of its individual reserves but, in the case of Broadland, to focus attention on the growing environmental problems resulting in part from changing agricultural practices. In 1976 the award-winning Ranworth Conservation Centre (now called the Broads Wildlife Centre) was opened. This floating building was erected on Swamp Carr, at the junction of Ranworth and Malthouse Broads, and could be approached by both land and water. The 500-metre walkway, bordered by descriptive panels, allowed visitors to see the changing flora from the oak woodlands of dry land to the reeds of the marsh at the broad's edge. Similar interpretive work and visitor facilities such as hides and leaflets were provided by the RSPB and the Nature Conservancy at other sites across Broadland.[10]

The importance of education had long been recognised by the National Trust at Blakeney Point and Scolt Head. As well as the field trips for university students from London and Cambridge, the post-war wardens Billy Eales and his son, Ted, introduced thousands of Norfolk children to the delights of the Point. These school excursions were part of the educational programme formulated by an advisory group under the chairmanship of Dr White of University College, London.[11]

It was not until the 1970s that the RSPB became involved in the acquisition of important sites in Norfolk. The first of these were the north Norfolk reserve at Titchwell and the Wash coast site at Snettisham, both in 1972. Two Broadland sites at Strumpshaw and Surlingham were added in 1975 and the Berney marshes ten years later. Finally, in 2006, Sutton Fen in the Broads was purchased.

The Broads Authority, too, has supported education facilities at How Hill with information panels at the staithe, a small museum in an eel-catcher's house and an electrically powered boat that takes visitors out on the river.

The importance of this increased interest in the countryside has also been appreciated by the Forestry Commission, who now see income from visitors forming a significant part of their business. Thetford Forest has an increasingly varied landscape as areas of conifer plantation give way to heathland, allowing for the natural regeneration of native species. Belts of beeches which were part of the original planting to provide fire breaks are now reaching maturity and visitors are encouraged to walk, cycle and visit historic sites within the forest. Access is open and free, but High Lodge is being developed as an increasingly popular visitor centre.

While much attention has been focused on the Broads, Breckland, the north Norfolk coast and the Wash, changes in farming across the county as a whole have been of great concern to conservationists. A particular issue has been the destruction of hedgerows and the infilling of marl pits. The brief for the Countryside Commission's *New Agricultural Landscapes*, published in 1972, had been to find out 'how agricultural improvement can be carried out efficiently but in such a way as to create new landscapes no less interesting than those destroyed in the process'. It revealed 'fresh and disturbing facts about the nature of change taking place', including the level of hedge destruction and the removal of field boundary trees, 90 per cent of which had gone since 1945. Wildlife habitats, too, were being destroyed by intensive farming. The creation of nature reserves and national parks was not enough. A balance between protection and productive use of the countryside as a whole needed to be found. The industrialisation of farming, rather than urbanisation, came to be seen as the greater threat to the appearance, wildlife and recreational value of the countryside.[12] Marion Shoard's book *The Theft of the Countryside* (1971) took up the themes of Nan Fairbrother and introduced the idea that farmers should be subjected to the same planning laws as everyone else. This view was promoted by the CPRE (of which Marion Shoard was secretary) in their report Landscape: the need for a public voice (1975). Farmers should be required to inform the local planning authority of their intention to remove hedges or plough up open heath. It also pressed for a package of tax relief to compensate for the loss of productivity that might result.

As always, it is only as the things we value begin to disappear that their importance is appreciated. It has already been shown how, encouraged by government subsidies, the 1960s saw the rapid increase in the intensification of farming and, with it, increasing publicity given to the damage to the rural environment. The response in the early 1970s saw these concerns being expressed in various ways in publications and particularly through the CPRE. The decade began with the European Year of the Environment and, in the UK, the creation of the Department of the Environment (DoE). In 1973 the Nature Conservancy was replaced by the Nature Conservancy Council (NCC) as a grant-aided body within the DoE. The decade also saw the beginnings of more militant movements attracting younger, more vociferous voices. Greenpeace was founded in 1970 and Friends of the Earth in 1971 with a membership of about 1,000. Ten years later membership of Friends of the Earth had risen to 27,000 and there were 200 active local groups. The Norfolk branch was frequently in evidence as the debates over the future of the Halvergate marshes grew more heated (see below). The Green Party was founded in 1973 and by the general election of 1989 received 15 per cent of the vote. Membership of such organisations as the National Trust, the NNT (now renamed the Norfolk Wildlife Trust (NWT)) and the RSPB also rose — in the case of the RSPB, from 10,500 in 1960 to 180,000 in 1974.[13] By 1995 10 per cent of the population belonged to an environmental group.

In 1973 the government set up the Countryside Review Committee to review the state of the countryside and the pressures upon it. In 1976 it produced a discussion paper, *The countryside: problems and policies*, which addressed the potential conflict between increasing food production and conservation. In 1977 a joint response from the National Farmers' Union (NFU) and Country Landowners' Association (CLA) was published with the title *Caring for the Countryside*, which gave practical advice on how farmers could combine food production with conservation.

One result of the growing realisation of the dangers of modern farming to a fragile ecological system, and particularly the need to safeguard wildlife habitats, was the Wildlife and Countryside Act of 1981, which heralded what John Sheail called 'the decade when it all happened'[14] — culminating, in 1987, with the publication of the Brundtland Report, *Our common future*, disseminating for the first time the concept of 'sustainable development'. The fact that the passing of the 1981 Act and the number of amendments tabled along the way was such a drawn-out process is an indication of how far the establishment still lagged behind public opinion. The scale of the vested interests of farmers and landowners, as well as a government which did not want to have to foot the bill for substantial compensation payments for farmers' loss of income for farming less intensively, was pitted against the conservationists. The bill is still the most

41 *The Friends of the Earth, under the local leadership of Andrew Lees, played an important role in ensuring the survival of the Halvergate marshes. Andrew later died while working in the Madagascan rain forest, but his significance for Halvergate is recorded in this stone at Wickhampton church.*

*Right: a cartoon by Tony Hall in the* Eastern Daily Press *on 15 June 1984 with the caption 'Let us pause children, to remember that gallant band of conservationists who fought on your behalf to preserve all this.'*

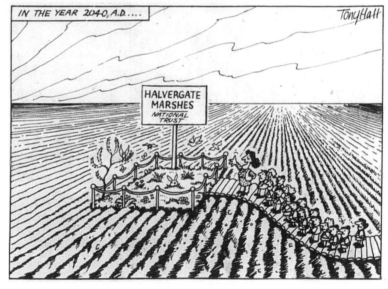

important piece of wildlife conservation legislation and it protects native species, including birds (and their nests and eggs), plants and animals, controls the release of non-native species, requires local authorities to compile maps of rights of way and gives greater protection for Sites of Special Scientific Interest (SSSIs). Importantly, it gave public authorities such as the recently established Broads Authority the right to negotiate management agreements with local farmers. The problem was that the cost of any such agreements had to be paid for by

42 *The demise of a drainage dyke near Tunstall Bridge, looking north-east towards the River Bure and Old Hall drainage mill. This traditional scene, from 1976, shows the grazed marsh with dyke sides well cropped by cattle. A few years later the wooden fence had been replaced by a metal one. By the early 1980s the field was arable and the dyke clogged with weeds now that the sides were no longer grazed. Finally, in the late 1980s, the ditch was filled in.*

the Authority and not the government (Ministry of Agriculture, Fisheries and Food (MAFF)).

International concern over the drainage of wetlands resulted in the Ramsar Convention, agreed in Iraq in 1971, by which wetlands of international significance were awarded special status. The first to be designated in Norfolk was the Ouse Washes in 1976, followed by Roydon Common in 1993, Breydon Water in 1996 and, more recently, Dersingham Bog, the north Norfolk coast, Broadland, and Redgrave and South Lopham fen. The draining of wetlands was becoming increasingly possible with new machinery, corrugated PVC piping for under-drainage and more powerful Archimedes screw-type pumps. This work was usually grant-aided by the Ministry of Agriculture and the impact of these advances was felt particularly on the broadland marshes. The only tool available in the 1970s to protect the area was the designation of the most significant sites as national nature reserves (NNRs) or Sites of Special Scientific Interest (SSSIs), and, as a result of pressure from the Broads Authority, the area of these rose from about 120 to 180 hectares between 1972 and 1981.[15] However, in many ways it was the large sweeps of the marshes that made them so significant in ecological and landscape terms and for these there could be little protection. The earliest large-scale drainage project in the Broads took place in the late 1970s and cov-

ered nearly 1,000 hectares to the south of the River Bure. The cost was over £400,000, which was mostly covered by grants, and the results allowed old grazing marshes to grow wheat and sugar beet. This intensity of arable farming not only removed wildlife habitats but also required the application of high levels of nitrogen, which soon seeped into the waterways, thus polluting them. The consequences for the landscape and ecology of the Bure valley were devastating, and fears for other areas of high amenity value were soon aroused. As a leader in the *Eastern Daily Press* put it in 1981:

> The history of the Broads over the last sixty years or so has been one of conflict – between exploitation and conservation – between urban and rural values – between various leisure groups – but perhaps above all, between those who want water and those who want rid of it. The lowering of the water table regardless of ecological changes resulting, continues almost inexorably, even it seems, under its latest guardians.[16]

As public concern mounted, the Broads Authority published a report in 1982 entitled *What Future for the Broads?* This graphically explained the consequences, in both landscape and ecological terms, of the drainage of grazing marshes and their conversion to arable.

Plans for other drainage schemes were soon put forward covering 3,635 hectares between the Rivers Yare and Bure, an area recognised by the Broads Authority as being 'probably the most important nationally, and also the most sensitive to change'.[17] It was the last remaining stretch of open grazing marsh in eastern England, 'wild, open, devoid of settlement and its varied ecology consisting of drainage dykes containing a fascinating variety of water plants, dragon

43 *A view across the Halvergate Marshes with Berney Arms windmill in the foreground and Breydon Water in the distance. The marshes represent the largest area of grazing marshes in England outside Somerset.*

flies and water beetles'.[18] For the first time the Broads Authority was in direct confrontation with farming interests and a rift appeared between some Authority members, often representing local farming and commercial interests, and their senior advisors, including their conservation officer, who regarded the damage to the distinctive character of the area as unacceptable. After some dithering and much lobbying by the CPRE and Friends of the Earth, the Authority resolved in February 1981 that the drainage scheme should be opposed and that negotiations with the local farmers and drainage boards on ways to keep the grazing marshes should continue. Meanwhile, Friends of the Earth kept up the pressure. In 1984 the debate moved to the national stage with a series of letters to *The Times*. The Norfolk landowner and Labour spokesman on conservation Lord Melchett initiated the correspondence with a letter on 6 February 1984 condemning hedge removal. The cause was taken up by Lord Buxton and Lord Onslow in a letter describing the Halvergate marshes as 'the largest remaining block of open marsh grazing landscape in England'. Their letter also pointed out the absurdity of paying farmers to drain and then compensating them not to drain.[19] Archaeologists, too, took up the cause, with Dr Martin Bell of Lampeter University highlighting the destruction of the historic countryside and the monuments within it. In a far-sighted contribution to the debate he called for an integrated approach to conservation and for protection for landscapes rather than individual monuments.[20] Lord Melchett expanded his views later in the year in a letter to the *Eastern Daily Press* calling for planning controls on change of use from pasture to arable on land that had not been ploughed for sixty years.[21]

In July 1984, in direct action supported by Lord Melchett, thirty people surrounded diggers and bulldozers in a quiet demonstration in Moulton St Mary, where drainage was planned on ninety acres of marsh. A letter was sent to the Prime Minister, Mrs Thatcher, asking that agricultural developments should be subject to planning control and that further deep drainage in marshland should be put on hold.[22] Further protests took place in Ludham and at St Benet's Abbey.[23] Members of the local branch of Friends of the Earth, under the leadership of Andrew Lees (later to lose his life while working for Friends of the Earth in the Madagascan rain forest), played an important role in keeping a look-out for any new drainage works. Twice they informed the Broads Authority of work about which they had not been notified. The *Eastern Daily Press* praised them for pursuing their objectives 'in the most direct and peaceful manner.'[24] The passing of the Wildlife and Countryside Act in 1981 allowed the Broads Authority to embark on an innovative experiment. By invoking Section 41 of the Act, the Authority required farmers to inform it of the intention to change grassland to arable. It was then up to the Authority to negotiate an agreement. As a result, the Broads Grazing Marshes Conservation Scheme was launched in 1985, which encouraged farmers in a tightly defined area enclosing the most sensitive grazing marshes around Halvergate to enter into management agreements to demonstrate how livestock farming and landscape preservation could work together. Subsidies of £50 a hectare were offered to participating farmers and a government grant was available to help underpin the scheme for three years. Farmers within the scheme were required to keep stocking rates low and consult the Authority before removing landscape or archaeological features, erecting buildings, constructing roads, underdraining, levelling or direct seeding the land and applying herbicides or anything but low levels of nitrogen. Here, for the first time nationally, we see farmers and conservationists working together to protect a unique landscape. It provided the model for the government's Environmentally Sensitive Areas (ESAs), introduced in the Agriculture Act of 1986, which accepted a statutory duty 'to achieve a reasonable balance between the promotion and maintenance of a stable and efficient agricultural industry and the conservation, amenity enhancement, wildlife, historic interest, public enjoyment, social and economic interests of the countryside'.[25] It allowed the government for the first time to channel agricultural money into conservation. The Broads were one of the first five ESAs to be established in England, with the scheme coming into operation in March 1986. This was a triumph for conservation, largely pioneered, often against much opposition, by the Broads Authority. It was immediately popular and has resulted in the inclusion by 2011 of 43,000 hectares of the grazing marshes, with their diverse and important wildlife and landscape remaining under traditional farming. Since 1985 the number of ESAs within the county has expanded to include the upper valleys of the Wensum and Bure and areas of Breckland. Alongside ESAs, Countryside Stewardship Schemes were introduced in 1991 to protect other farmland of environmental significance. The two separate schemes are now (2014) being gradually phased out and replaced by Higher Level Stewardship schemes to protect farmland of wildlife and historic importance.

While these voluntary agreements form an essential part of conservation in Broadland and elsewhere, closely monitored and protected areas remains important. As farmers came to realise that the ploughing up of the marsh was not likely to be acceptable they began, in some cases, to put land up for sale, and in 1986 the RSPB bought land in the Halvergate marshes from the Berney estate and the Berney Marshes Nature Reserve was established. Its holding has since been increased to 1,000 acres. Water levels are carefully managed by blocking off the end of ditches to stop the water running off the reserves, while traditional windmills stop the water levels rising too high. As a result the number of breeding wading birds has increased, peaking at 324 pairs in 2008, while the number of wintering wildfowl on the marshes and neighbouring Breydon Water has also gone up dramatically. The RSPB also works with neighbouring farmers so that an area covering 6,000 acres is farmed in order to provide an extended habitat for waders.

As well as the highly publicised conflicts, more considered discussions were

44  *Emily Swan of Natural England speaking about rare flowering plants growing in arable fields on a FWAG walk at Peewit Farm, Briston, in July 2010.*

under way. It was clear that a multi-use principle had to be established whereby, on land that was not designated as of special interest or value, concessions were still made to the natural and cultural environment. While designated areas are essential for providing habitats for rare species, the more common ones need protecting in the wider countryside. Specialist conservation was required on protected sites, while, elsewhere, farmers and landowners could complement them in supporting more common species, which also form essential parts of the eco-system. The late 1960s saw exercises at the Farmers' Weekly farm at Tring to discover practical ways of combining conservation with profitable farming. This led to the founding of the first Farming and Wildlife Advisory Group (FWAG). At first this was little more than a national talking shop for the main organisations involved with the management of land, with MAFF acting as the secretariat, but this soon developed, with the founding of local FWAGs at county level. In

1983 a meeting was held at Sennowe Hall in Norfolk, hosted by the then chairman of the NWT and attended by the Duchess of Kent, to which landowners, farmers and other potential benefactors were invited. The aim was to consider how to start a local FWAG and to fund a Norfolk FWAG adviser. This resulted in the setting up of a system of part-time voluntary advisers from the RSPB, the Agricultural Development Advisory Service (ADAS) and the County Council ecologist working with local farmers. The national Farming and Wildlife Trust was founded in 1984 and supported by MAFF, ADAS and the NFU, as well as a membership of farmers. This enabled the funding of local advisors and the first full-time FWAG adviser funded by MAFF and ADAS was appointed to work alongside the volunteers.[26] Soon there were sixty-two county FWAGs with over thirty full-time advisors. As well as advising individual farmers they ran seminars and organised farm walks (the first in Norfolk, soon after the appointment of the full-time adviser, was to Abbots Farm, Stoke Holy Cross) which provided useful meeting places for like-minded individuals. From being a talking shop, FWAG became a co-operative agency for promoting good conservation practice on working farms.[27]

More recently it has been positive steps to restore diversity that have been of increasing importance. For instance, the water of many of the Broads, such as Barton Broad, has been invaded by algae, mainly as a result of the enrichment of the water by phosphates and nitrates. The algae have blocked out sunlight, causing many plants to die and sink to the bottom, forming a thick muddy deposit. However, programmes of dredging have pumped out huge quantities of sludge and encouraged the return of waterfleas, which eat algae, and so the water has become clear again, resulting in a return of a diversity of animal and plant life.

## Archaeological remains

So far concern over the destruction of natural habitats and diversity had been the major concern. However, not only were habitats in the farmed landscape under threat but so was the archaeology. Realisation of the pressures modern farming put on archaeology led the government to set up the Walsh Committee to report on the management of field monuments, the findings of which were published in 1969.[28] The report made several important recommendations including the appointment of Field Monument Wardens to conduct regular inspections and the compiling of local records of monuments for the information of local planning authorities. The damage done by ploughing, the flattening of earthworks and the grubbing up of woodland was soon appreciated as a real danger. In 1971 (the same year as the founding of Friends of the Earth) archaeologists, spurred on initially by the destruction of urban sites under new development, founded Rescue.

One of the stated aims of Rescue was to encourage the creation of the post of County Archaeologist. The Norfolk Archaeological Unit, founded in 1973 and taken over by the County Council in 1978, was run by the County Archaeologist within the county Museum Service. It was the first such county-based unit to be formed in Britain, responding to one of the recommendation of the Walsh Committee. It built on previous records kept by the museum to create a County Sites and Monuments Record (SMR). The Unit was responsible for initiating several county surveys of monuments which were a necessary precursor to evaluating monuments to be recommended for protection. These reports were published in a new series, entitled *East Anglian Archaeology*, launched by Norfolk and Suffolk County Councils in 1975. These included surveys of barrows in East Anglia (1981), ruined and disused churches of Norfolk (1991) and earthworks in Norfolk (2003). The barrow survey was the first comprehensive survey of a particular class of monument in the country, resulting in the scheduling of all Norfolk's well-preserved examples. While the survey of all earthworks in grassland in the county did not result in newly identified sites receiving statutory protection it is regularly referred to by farmers and their advisors to ensure sites are recognised in ESAs and other Stewardship schemes. The ruined churches survey provided a useful catalogue of surviving ruins in a county that has more such sites than any other in England. At the same time, new sites were being identified by air photography. For instance, while 196 flattened Bronze Age burial mounds had been recorded by 1974, air photography resulted in 712 new ones being located by 1986. By 1987, the Archaeological Unit air photograph library held over 21,500 photographs.[29]

A report by English Heritage in 1995 entitled *The Monuments at Risk Survey*

(MARS) pointed to the destruction caused by modern farming. Nationally, for the period 1945-1995, the percentage of earthwork monuments with very good survival had fallen by 20 per cent, and other figures were equally dramatic. Although these figures cover England as a whole, it was in the arable east that destruction was greatest.[30]

## 'Preservation by record'

Some of the greatest threats to archaeology came from urban regeneration and here the only possibility was to excavate and record before sites were destroyed ('preservation by record'). Following a visit to Kings Lynn by the Society for Medieval Archaeology in 1962, 1963 saw the start of the Kings Lynn Survey. Largely supported by the Ministry of Works, a series of rescue excavations within the old town took place from 1963 to 1971. Alongside the excavations went a study of standing buildings and documentary work – a model example of coordinated research which has been published.[31] This was followed by the Norwich Survey, funded by the Department of the Environment, Norwich City Council and Norfolk County Council and supported by the University of East Anglia. Between 1971 and 1978 thirty-eight sites were excavated, accompanied by architectural and documentary research. The aim was to 'record and publish evidence for the origin and development of the city'.[32]

Encouraged by these heightened programmes of research, in March 1988 strong policies for conserving the county's archaeology were introduced into Norfolk's *Structure Plan*, which stated that 'Development which would affect sites of outstanding archaeological importance will only be permitted in exceptional circumstances. On other sites of archaeological importance and where there is no overriding case for preservation, development will not normally be permitted unless agreement has been reached to provide for the recording and, where desirable, the excavation of such sites.'[33] These two policies were a great leap forward and provided for the first time strong grounds for recommending the refusal of planning permission for archaeological reasons and for arguing the case for developer funding of excavations in the affected area in return for planning consent. The first excavation paid for in this way pre-dated the County

Structure Plan by nearly ten years. In 1979 Anglia Television wished to extend their offices within the area of the north-east bailey of Norwich Castle, which was a Scheduled Ancient Monument. The 1979 Ancient Monuments and Archaeological Areas Act, which would have the power to prevent the destruction of a scheduled site, was then being discussed by parliament, and as a result tough negotiations took place and the company agreed to pay for the excavation. This excavation showed that before the area had been cleared by the Normans there had been a church with a large cemetery on the site. Long before the days of Time Team, this work received much television coverage and was described in a popular booklet, *Digging under the Doorstep*.[34] In 1987 a further development within the Castle outer bailey was proposed – the Castle Mall shopping centre – and, again, the developer agreed to pay for excavation. The result was a large-scale excavation funded by the developer in 1987-1991.[35] As with the Anglia Television site, a great effort was made to engage the public by providing a viewing platform and exhibition, while school parties were encouraged to visit.

A further cause of destruction of archaeological sites was road improvement. This included the proposed A140 Scole bypass, which ran through a Roman town, while a series of sites were threatened by the A47 Norwich southern bypass. In both cases the Department of Transport agreed to finance survey and, where necessary, excavations – and in both cases before the law required them to do so.[36]

Although already foreshadowed by statements in the Norfolk *Structure Plan*, 1990 saw an important national initiative for the protection of archaeological sites with the publication of Planning Policy Guidance 16 (PPG 16), 'Archaeology and Planning'. This stated that 'Where nationally important archaeological remains, whether scheduled or not, and their settings, are affected by proposed development, there should be a presumption in favour of their physical preservation.' For the first time unscheduled sites could be protected as well as scheduled ones and, as with wildlife, there was the realisation that the drawing of tight boundaries around a protected area was not the way forward. The destruction of its setting could be equally damaging. PPG 16 also introduced nationally something already accepted in Norfolk: the concept of 'preservation by record', whereby, if the case for development outweighed that for preservation, then the planning authority could insist that the site was archaeologically recorded and a full record made at the expense of the developer before any new work was undertaken. The first brief issued by Norfolk Landscape Archaeology (the renamed Norfolk Archaeological Unit) on behalf of the County Council was in March 1991. It required the developer of an area of housing in a field on the edge of Watton adjacent to a Roman road where there was evidence for Roman-British settlement to appoint an archaeological contractor to undertake a small excavation sampling 2 per cent of the area and produce a report of the findings.

Although this control of destruction as a result of development was a start, the reduction in the destruction caused by the ploughing up of grassland and gradual attrition of sites on arable land had to await the agri-environment schemes of the 1990s. Even today many archaeological sites of importance remain unscheduled and continue to be ploughed and subsoiled with no protection whatsoever.

## The protection and care of churches

'Norfolk is one of the architectural treasures of Europe because of its medieval country churches. Their *profusion* is their greatness.'[37] So wrote John Betjeman in 2001 on the subject of a further area of concern, the future of some of Norfolk's 659 medieval churches, many of them remote from their communities. In 1972 the Norfolk Society (the local branch of the CPRE), on behalf of their Committee for Country Churches, published *Norfolk Country Churches and the Future*. Edited by Lady Wilhemena Harrod (one of the authors of the Shell Guide), the foreword was written by John Betjeman. The Pastoral Measure of 1968 ('one of the most complicated pieces of ecclesiastical legislation of recent years'[38]) allowed for the Diocesan Pastoral Committees to recommend to the Church Commissioners churches to be declared redundant. As a result, after consultation with the Redundant Churches Advisory Boards, some might be converted to other uses, while the most architecturally important could be taken over by the Redundant Churches Fund, who would be responsible for their repair and maintenance. By 1976 the Committee for Country Churches had become the Norfolk Churches Trust (the first such trust in the country), with Lady Harrod as its first chairman. Its aim was to prevent redundancies by encouraging interest in the county's churches, declaring that 'every church in the county is of value for its part in the life of the community, its effect on the landscape, and its interesting features'.[39] From the beginning, the Trust organised church tours which usually attracted over a hundred people. The Trust encourages a membership and receives grants, particularly from the Government's landfill Tax Credit Scheme, which enable it to give advice and financial help. Not only was the Trust a first for the country, but so was its annual sponsored cycle ride, in which participants cycle to as many churches as they can in one day. This usually raises over £100,000 and is an idea which had been taken up elsewhere. During the first twenty-five years of its work the Trust rescued twenty-five churches from closure after periods of disuse and decay, as well as grant-aiding essential repair work in many others.[40]

## The protection and management of field monuments

As with wildlife, there was a need for a more positive approach to the protection of field monuments involving a joint approach between farmers and archaeologists. Under Section 17 of the Ancient Monuments and Archaeological Areas Act of 1979 grant-aided management agreements were made available to owners and occupiers of ancient monuments, and until 1990 these were always directly initiated by English Heritage and were mostly for scheduled monuments. However, there was a need to alert farmers to the valuable historical evidence on their land and to its fragility. In the late 1980s a booklet called 'Farming on ancient monuments in Norfolk' was published and distributed by ADAS. In 1990 a new project, The Norfolk Monuments Management Project (NMMP), was piloted in Norfolk, whereby the County Council's Department of Planning and Transportation and the renamed Field Archaeology Division of the Museum Service took over from English Heritage the role of offering Section 17 grants. This initiative was the first of its kind in Britain and a NMMP officer was appointed by and reported to a committee chaired by the County Archaeologist and representing farming, wildlife and archaeological interests. An important feature of the early years was a six-monthly meeting of the committee, which would include a field visit. This helped all involved to understand the issues and it enthused them with a love of history and a wish to protect sites on farms. The

*45 The demolition of a Norman house in Queen Street, Kings Lynn, in 1977 drew national attention to the lack of protection for many such buildings. Shown here are workmen chipping off the stucco (right) to reveal two Norman windows (opposite top) and the overnight demolition of the building (opposite below).*

work of the project officer involved arranging visits to farms where a field monument had been identified through previous survey. Unlike the practice under English Heritage, the scheme was promoted among farmers of unscheduled (but believed to be of schedulable quality) as well as scheduled sites. In this way awareness of the significance of sites was raised and many farmers were happy to enter into management agreements funded by English Heritage and to consult the NMMP officer on suitable farming methods to protect the monument. Links with FWAG have ensured an integrated approach to archaeology and wildlife.[41]

## The protection of historic buildings

The early 1970s saw concern over the inadequate coverage of the early lists of historic buildings, which had been very selective in the types of buildings covered. Very few built since 1830 were included, so many early industrial buildings, as well as Victorian and twentieth-century buildings, were left unrecognised. The lack of descriptions also reduced the value of the early lists. Many buildings had also been missed and these sometimes came to light only when work on alteration or demolition began. In this case, emergency 'spot-listing' was possible to halt the work. Builders who suspected that spot-listing might be contemplated, however, could simply demolish before a notification came

*46 The grade I sixteenth-century Waxham barn was compulsorily purchased by the Norfolk County Council to save it from collapse. With funding from a variety of sources it has been restored to its former glory.*

through. Nationally, the weekend demolition in 1980 of the Firestone building, a distinctive modernist building of the 1930s on the Great West Road in London, hit the headlines. Locally, a Norman house in Queens Street, Kings Lynn, previously unrecognised behind a stucco façade, was demolished over a weekend in 1977 when a spot-listing request was likely to be enforced on the Monday. Although the building was in a Conservation Area and early photographs showed the outline of Norman windows before the building was refaced, its importance had not been fully appreciated or researched before a public enquiry and permission for demolition had been granted.

As a result of such cases, a national resurvey to update the lists was begun by inspectors from the Ministry of Works. Progress was slow and by 1980 only towns and the former Rural District of Depwade in the south of the county had been covered. In 1980 Michael Heseltine, the then Minister for the Environment, realised that at this rate it would take centuries to complete the work and so introduced the 'accelerated resurvey'. In Norfolk three new staff on three-year contracts were attached to the county conservation team to undertake the work. Descriptions were much more detailed and photographic slides of every building were taken, which are still held by the county's planning department. While there were certainly some buildings that slipped through the net, particularly in the Depwade area, which had been re-covered in the 1970s, the resulting coverage led to an increased awareness of the great wealth of historic buildings in the county and its rich architectural heritage. The lists now cover 11,203 buildings, ranging from small structures such as lime kilns and pig sties to great houses such as Holkham Hall. Part IV of the 1968 Town and Country Planning Act had introduced both spot-listing, a vital defence against premature demolition, and the listed building consent procedure, which required planning authorities to consider application for demolition or alteration against a specific set of criteria. There should always be a presumption in favour of preservation unless there was a strong case for demolition. However, the fine for illegal demolition was less than £100, which was hardly a deterrent to an impatient developer. A *Buildings at Risk Register* is produced every year both locally, by the County Council, and nationally, by English Heritage, and includes all grade I and II* buildings that face particular threats from either unsuitable redevelopment or dereliction. In 1984 English Heritage, a government quango which took over the roles of the Historic Buildings Council and the Ancient Monuments Board and the responsibilities for the historic fabric which had been part of the Department of the Environment, was created. It became the statutory advisor to the Department of the Environment on such matters as listing and scheduling.

The county's regularly updated *Buildings at Risk Register* was an important tool for conservationists, as was shown in the case of the gigantic grade I listed sixteenth-century barn at Waxham, which had become increasingly dilapidated since 1950. The great October gales of 1987 blew away much of what remained of its roof and the owner applied for consent to demolish, which was refused; when he failed to comply with a Repairs Notice the County Council acquired it

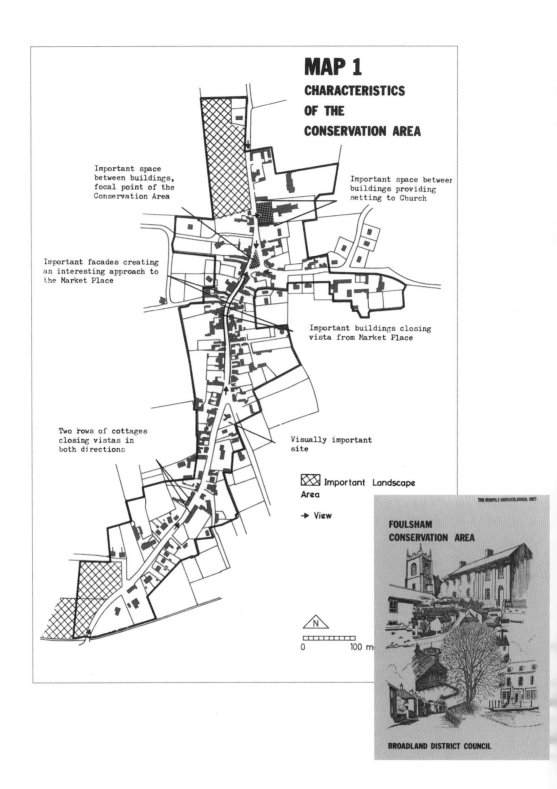

**MAP 1**

**CHARACTERISTICS OF THE CONSERVATION AREA**

Important space between buildings, focal point of the Conservation Area

Important space between buildings providing setting to Church

Important facades creating an interesting approach to the Market Place

Important buildings closing vista from Market Place

Two rows of cottages closing vistas in both directions

Visually important site

⊠ Important Landscape Area

→ View

N

0          100 m

FOULSHAM CONSERVATION AREA

THE NORFOLK ARCHAEOLOGICAL UNIT

BROADLAND DISTRICT COUNCIL

*47  Foulsham Conservation Area: Foulsham was one of the earliest
conservation areas to be designated (1979). As a result the historic
core has retained much of its traditional character.*

by compulsory purchase. With funding from a variety of sources, repair work took place between 1991 and 1993 at a cost of just under £500,000. It now stands rethatched, weatherproof and repaired, and is a fine example of sixteenth-century decorative brickwork within flint walling.

In the early 1990s the County Council produced a series of 'Topic papers' covering various types of buildings, such as ruined churches, drainage mills, corn mills and farm buildings. This resulted in thirteen ruined churches being repaired and consolidated between 1992 and 1997 with funds from the County Council and English Heritage. The most dramatic of these projects was the saving of the little church of Houghton-on-the-Hill, with its wealth of unique and beautiful wall paintings, the earliest dating from the late eleventh century.[42]

## The protection of villages

With the exception of villages on the outskirts of Norwich, Great Yarmouth and Kings Lynn, the population of a total of 483 parishes fell by nearly 10,000 in the 1950s. By 1966 the number of villages in decline had reduced to 300. In 1968 the County Council received a report from the County Planning Officer entitled 'The Dying Village'.[43] The disappearance of jobs in agriculture coupled with the closure of local railways and RAF bases led to the steady run-down of local services. At the same time the ability of townspeople to travel ever-further to work meant that during the 1960s villages were ceasing to be focused on farming, and instead becoming commuter communities. Older village properties were being bought up and there was often a rapid increase of modern housing around historic cores. Old sets of farm buildings became redundant and either fell into ruin or were converted, sometimes unsympathetically, into desirable 'executive' residences. The attractions of living in the countryside also appealed to those reaching retirement age. Selling an urban property and exchanging it for a new bungalow with a garden on the edge of an old village could be a financially attractive proposition. Pressure groups and local residents' associations (frequently made up of incomers) sprang up to prevent the onrush of change. 'Articulate and influential, the newcomers were able to ensure that local planning policies reflect[ed] their views.'[44] The need to protect not only individual historic buildings but also whole neighbourhoods resulted in the concept of 'conservation areas', created under the Civic Amenities Act of 1967, which aimed 'to make provision for the protection and improvement of buildings of agricultural or historic interest and of the character of areas of such interest'. It recognised the importance of preserving the harmony of whole areas rather than individual buildings in isolation. Pleasant groups of buildings together with open spaces, trees, historic street patterns and village greens were recognised as all contributing to the special character of an area. The act allowed local authorities, after consultation with local communities, to designate such areas where stricter planning controls would be implemented. However, the legislation lacked teeth and it was not until the Town and Country Amenities Act of 1974 that permission was required to demolish an unlisted building in a Conservation Area. Norfolk was slow to designate Conservation Areas but in 1971 a list of fifty-nine towns and villages for study and potential designation was drawn up, with Woodbastwick in the Broads to be the first to be designated. It was quickly followed by many more in both village and urban situations. In the 1980s and 1990s rural conservation areas began to be established, such as one in the Glaven Valley and later the Halvergate marshes, and, even more recently, Coltishall RAF base. The mid-1970s also saw the first conservation officers to be appointed by district councils in Norfolk. The downside of this was that conservation could be seen as a negative movement, preventing progress and strangling the countryside. Indeed, although Conservation Areas often created a new awareness of and pride in the built environment within the community, in practice they could do little other than discourage the demolition of historic buildings in town and village centres.

In 1974 local government was reorganised and the County Council now had strategic planning and transportation responsibilities over the whole county. The statutory plan-making process started afresh, with a Norfolk Structure Plan approved in 1978. The new Districts were responsible for local planning decisions in line with the requirements of the Structure Plan and there was much more emphasis on environmental protection and building conservation.[45]

*48  One of the first projects of the Norfolk Buildings Trust was the restoration of the two lodges designed by John Soane at the entrance to Langley Park, just outside Chedgrave.*

## The Norfolk County Council-sponsored Trusts

In the late 1970s it was apparent that many important Norfolk buildings of architectural and historic merit were becoming derelict, either because their owners refused to sell them or because prospective purchasers regarded them as uneconomic. To address this situation the County Council's planning and transportation department initiated the creation of various trusts which would be in a position to attract outside funding. To coincide with European Architectural Heritage Year in 1975, the government established an Architectural Heritage Fund

from which such trusts could borrow money at low interest rates to tackle repair projects that would otherwise be unviable.

The first such trust in Norfolk was the Norfolk Historic Buildings Trust, set up jointly by Norfolk County Council and the Norfolk Society. The Trust acquired its first property in 1978 and has since operated on the 'revolving fund' principle. However, where buildings could not be converted without losing their essential conservation value, they have been retained by the Trust. The Norfolk Windmills Trust was also established to help conserve the mills and pumps that are a distinctive feature of the county's heritage. Such initiatives demonstrate

49 *How Hill windmill was restored with the help of a grant from the Norfolk Windmills Trust.*

the significant role of voluntary and charitable bodies, particularly when public sector resources are scarce, if the distinctiveness of the local environment is to be conserved. The 1970s saw the County Council increasingly involved with conservation of both buildings and landscapes. As well as supporting the Buildings and Windmill Trusts, its Planning and Transportation Department took on wider responsibilities for the countryside as a whole. In 1975 the Landscape Conservation Programme was launched with the aim of enhancing the appearance and condition of the countryside. Its first concern was the loss of trees and it provided advice as well as Landscape Conservation grants for farmland tree planting. However, by 1999 'developing ideas in conservation' had resulted in extending the programme to include meadows, grasslands, heathlands, river valleys, historic parklands and other historic landscapes. The concept of encouraging 'a sense of place' and the 'whole farm/holding' approach in the different regions of Norfolk entered the terminology. Woodland in the form of copses, scrub, hedgerows, avenues, beech and pine belts, river valleys, ponds, historic parklands and commons were also now to be valued and their maintenance in good condition was eligible, if nothing else was available, for County Council grants. The importance of working in partnership with the various voluntary organisations and governmental departments was recognised.[46] From 1997 Hedgerow Regulations had made it illegal to destroy a hedgerow if it was more than twenty metres in length or over thirty years old and the local authority was the enforcement authority.

## The other county Trusts

The challenges presented by the pressures on both the natural and cultural environment described above meant that there was plenty for both the NWT and the NAT to be concerned about. With the rapidly increasing membership of the NWT described above (35,000 by 2012), and with successful appeals for funds, further purchases of land were possible. While original acquisitions had concentrated very much on the north Norfolk coast and the Broads, with smaller areas in Breckland, other types of habitat were increasingly recognised as being under threat. Commons and woodland were added. In 1973 the cartoonist Osbert

50　*The ancient woodland at Foxley was purchased by the NWT in 1989. Bluebells flourish amongst the pollarded hazels.*

Lancaster gave the Trust East Winch Common. The two ancient woodlands of Wayland (1975) and Foxley (1989), became Trust property later. The Woodland Trust, founded 1972, has acquired Tyrrels Wood and other Norfolk sites. As well as owning sites, the NWT leases and manages other areas. One of its most unusual sites is the railway line at Narborough in west Norfolk, where the digging of cuttings has created an important chalkland habitat. The Trust now (2014) owns or manages thirty-eight different reserves. The emphasis has now moved from the acquisition of isolated areas to connecting sites to provide corridors between existing reserves. This policy has allowed the area of land owned

*51 The central area of Caistor Roman Town was given to the Norfolk Archaeological Trust in a bequest in 1984. Additional land was purchased in 1991/92 and 2011 to include much of the extra-mural settlement surrounding the town. The Roman street pattern can be clearly seen in the grass in dry weather.*

around the Cley marshes to be greatly expanded as well as new acquisitions made linking several broads. The Trust now owns or manages 4,300 hectares. The Living Landscapes initiative involves working with partners across wider areas to give wildlife space to survive and adapt to change. As we have seen, the importance of interpretation and engaging the public has also been actively addressed. From its original centre at Ranworth, there are now visitor centres at Cley, Hickling, Holme and Weeting, with a board walk at Barton Broad and Thompson Common.

Unlike the NWT, the NAT has been hampered by a shortage of members

(there are still fewer than 100), but it has been very successful in recent years in attracting grants for purchase and interpretation. The introduction of agri-environment schemes has allowed sites which are purchased to be taken out of the plough, thus preventing further damage from both ploughing and illegal metal detecting. They are then put into an Environmental Stewardship Scheme which provides funds for their future management. Following its early acquisitions, described in a previous chapter, it was not until 1984 that any more properties were added. In that year, however, the central area of Caistor Roman town, surrounded by its late Roman defences, was given to the Trust. This scheduled site

52 *Recent Heritage Lottery Funded work at St Benet's Abbey by the Norfolk Archaeological Trust has involved new interpretation panels, one showing a reconstruction of the site (left) overlaying an aerial photograph as it is today (above).*

had already been removed from cultivation in 1973, but much of the Roman town lay outside the bequest and there was no vehicular access. Additional land was purchased in 1991 and 1992 with English Heritage and local authority funding. The holding now consisted of forty-nine hectares and was immediately put down to grass to prevent erosion of the archaeology by ploughing and sub-soiling. A car park for twenty-five cars was constructed and waymarked walks around the Roman defences and beside the neighbouring river were created, with a series of information panels beside the paths. A leaflet and site guide books are available in local shops. It was one of the first large areas to be put into a Stewardship Scheme, and was opened to the public by the chairman of the Countryside Commission in 1993. The project received five national awards over the next two years. In 2011 a further large field across the river containing an area of extra-mural settlement and Saxon occupation was purchased with the aid of funds from the National Memorial Fund (the first time a grant was given for the purchase of land). Other purchases included the Tasburgh Iron Age enclosure (1994), the Saxon Shore fort at Burgh Castle (1995), the addition of the priory gatehouse and adjoining field at Binham Priory (2003 and 2005), St Benet's Abbey (2002–04), South Creake Iron Age fort (2003), Burnham Norton gatehouse and priory site (2011) and, finally, Fiddler's Hill barrow (2012). All these sites are managed with wildlife as well as archaeology in mind.

## The future

Where does this leave the conservation movement today? From its early beginnings in the nineteenth century to the 1950s the movement can be seen as an exclusive one, supported by minority interest groups such as naturalists, archaeologists and architectural historians. The emphasis was very much on the preservation and protection of rare and exceptional sites. However, one result of improved standards of living and leisure opportunities, helped very much by mass communication and the spread of the motor car, has been the increasing awareness of and public interest in all aspects of the countryside. The conservation groups have responded to this by opening up their sites and introducing educational programmes. The importance of the typical as well as the exceptional has become understood and the emphasis has moved away from 'preservation' to 'conservation', and more recently, in planning terms, 'regeneration'. Protection is not seen necessarily as negative and restrictive but, as in the case of FWAG and NMMP, as a partnership of interests between those who work the land and those who wish to protect its historical and ecological assets. The importance of diversity in ecological terms is better understood and is becoming more generally accepted in the farming community and encouraged through environmental grant schemes such as that pioneered in the Norfolk Broads. The closing down of much of the countryside to visitors during the foot and mouth outbreak of 2001 showed how important tourism was to the rural economy. The attraction of the countryside relies very much on its variety of flora and fauna as well as its historic and landscape interest. The early twenty-first century has seen the replacement of previous crop and livestock payments, which had linked production and financial support. Instead, under the Single Farm Payment Scheme farmers are paid by the acreage they farm and have to demonstrate that they are keeping land in 'Good agricultural and environmental condition'. This discourages the ploughing up of permanent grassland and ensures that SSSIs and Scheduled Ancient Monuments are protected.[47]

Much of this new thinking on conservation was reflected in Planning Policy Guidance 15 (PPG15), published in 2002 and entitled 'Planning and the Historic Environment'. The importance of a partnership between local authorities, private individuals and businesses, as well as conservation bodies, is understood. The importance of education that emphasises the value of the natural and cultural landscapes is recognised as being an essential ingredient in the promotion of conservation. The significance of both the 'wider historic landscape' and the importance of conservation to tourism and regeneration is stressed. 'Policies to strengthen the rural economy through environmentally sensitive diversification may be among the most important for its conservation.'[48]

In just over a century the legal protection of historic sites and monuments has moved from being voluntary to a far more complicated situation which recognises that such sites have a national significance which can override private ownership. Local planning authorities now have an important role in the protection of both ecologically and archaeologically sensitive sites, while at the same time acknowledging the importance of working with other interested parties. Through full consultation, together with positive and informed negotiation, conflict can be avoided and a compromise which suits all concerned can be achieved.

While the future for the natural and much of the cultural heritage in Norfolk looks positive as a result of partnerships between conservationists, on the one hand, and owners, farmers and developers, on the other, the outlook for much of the built environment is less rosy. Heritage protection is frequently regarded with suspicion. It is often seen as an 'opposition movement ... fighting against weather, time, decay, greed, ignorance, funding cuts, development pressures,

Government policy …. Battling to stop bad things happening to the heritage … a position inherently weak and reactive and crucially (unlike those working for the natural heritage) we haven't been able to get the message across to the larger public'.[49] Listing is often seen as a negative move, to such an extent that it can stifle good modern architecture because developers do not want buildings that might end up listed, thus constraining what can be done to them at a later date.[50] While the 'heritage industry' is being increasingly recognised as central to the economy of the countryside, government funding for historic buildings is declining.

However, to end on a more optimistic note, many of the conservation initiatives described in this book were pioneered in Norfolk, from the founding of the Wildlife and Archaeological Trusts in the 1920s to the forerunners of Environmentally Sensitive Areas in the Norfolk Broads in the 1970s and the Norfolk Monument Management Project in the 1990s. As a county traditionally associated with intensive farming, alongside some of the most important wetlands and coastal areas for wildlife in Britain, and with a history which saw it as the country's most prosperous and populous region from the Iron Age through to the Middle Ages, there is much to conserve. Initiatives which see the rich diversity of Norfolk's landscape valued and cared for by those who live and work here, and enjoyed by the many who visit, should continue to be a key element in planning for the county's future.

1    Lowe 1986, 55.
2    Scott 1942, *passim*.
3    H. Newby (1988) *The countryside in question*. London, Hutchison, 73.
4    Norfolk County Council 1994, 20-21.
5    Oxford Archaeological Unit (1999) *Management of archaeological sites in arable landscapes*. Oxford, OAU, 5 and 37; Lawson 1981, 34-35.
6    Norfolk County Council, Broads Consortium (1971) *Broadland study and plan*. Norwich, NCC.
7    C. Chinery (1999) 'Population', in T. Heaton (ed.), Norfolk century. Norwich, *Eastern Daily Press*, 26-7.
8    D.N. Jeans (1990) 'Planning and the myth of the English countryside', *Rural History* 1, 261.

9    D. Matless, C. Watkins and P. Merchant (2010) 'Nature Trails: the production of an instructive landscape in Britain', *Rural History* 21:1, 97-131.

10   George 1992, 476-8.

11   Allison and Morley 1989, 10.

12   Sheail 1998, 210.

13   Sheail 1976, 228.

14   Sheail 1998, 165.

15   George 1992, 481.

16   *Eastern Daily Press*, 26 January 1981.

17   George 1992, 282.

18   Lowe 1986, 268.

19   *The Times*, 18 February 1984.

20   *The Times*, 11 February 1984.

21   *Eastern Daily Press*, 16 July 1984.

22   *Eastern Daily Press*, 3 July 1984.

23   *Eastern Daily Press*, 21 July and 15 August 1984.

24   Lowe 1986, 297; *Eastern Daily Press*, 18 August 1984.

25   Sheail 1998, 242.

26   Pers. comm. Peter Grimble and Greg Pritchard.

27   N.W. Moore (1987) *The bird of time: the science and politics of nature conservation - a personal account*. Cambridge, Cambridge University Press, 107.

28   Parliamentary Papers (1966-68) Report of the Committee of Enquiry into the arrangements for the protection of field monuments (The Walshe Report), Command Paper 3904, London, HMSO.

29   D.A. Edwards and P. Wade-Martins (1987) *Norfolk from the Air*. Norwich, Norfolk Museums Service, 9-10.

30   Bournemouth University and English Heritage (1995) *The Monuments at Risk Survey of England*. London, English Heritage, 11.

31   H. Clarke and A. Carter (1977) *Excavations in Kings Lynn 1963-1970*, Society for Medieval Archaeology Monograph 7. London, Society for Medieval Archaeology; D.M. Owen (1984) *The making of Kings Lynn: a documentary survey*. Oxford, Oxford University Press for the British Academy; V. Parker (1971) *The making of Kings Lynn: secular buildings from the 11th to the 17th century*. Chichester, Phillimore.

32   M. Atkin et al. (1982) *Excavations in Norwich 1971-1978*, Part 1. East Anglian Archaeology 15, Norwich, Norwich Survey in conjunction with the Scole Archaeological Committee, 1.

33   Wade-Martins 1999, 310-11.

34   B. Ayers and A. Lawson (1983) *Digging under the doorstep*. Norwich, Norfolk Museum Service; B. Ayres (1985) *Excavations within the north-east bailey of Norwich Castle, 1979*. East Anglian Archaeology 28, Norwich, Norfolk Museum Service.

35   B. Ayers, J. Bown and J. Reeve (1992) *Digging Ditches*. Norwich, Norfolk Museum Service. S. Popescu (2009) *Norwich Castle: excavations and historical survey, 1987-1998*, parts 1 and 2. East Anglian Archaeology 9, Gressenhall, Norfolk Museums Service, 132.

36   T. Ashwin, S. Bates and K. Penn (2000) *Norwich southern bypass, excavations 1989-1991*, parts 1 and 2 East Anglian Archaeology 91, Gressenhall, Norfolk Museum Service.

37  J. Betjeman (2001) 'A greatness in profusion', in C. Roberts (ed.), *Treasure for the Future*. Norwich, Norfolk Churches Trust, 1.

38  P. Paget (1972) 'How the Scheme for Redundant Churches is meant to work', in W. Harrod (ed.), *Norfolk Country Churches and the Future*. Holt, The Norfolk Society, 16.

39  Aims of the Norfolk Churches Trust as listed on the back of R. Greenwood and M. Norris (1976) *The brasses of Norfolk churches*. Norwich, Norfolk Churches Trust.

40  For a general survey of the Trust's work see C. Roberts (ed.) (2001) *Treasure for the future: a celebration of the Norfolk Churches Trust 1976-2001*. Norwich, Norfolk Churches Trust.

41  H. Paterson and P. Wade-Martins (1999) 'Monument conservation in Norfolk', in J. Grenville (ed.), *Managing the historic rural landscape*. London, Routledge, 137-48.

42  http://www.hoh.org.uk

43  J. Ayton (2013) 'The first county development plan; part 2, after the plan 1951-71', *The Annual* 22, 5-19.

44  Newby 1988, 40.

45  Ayton 2013, 19.

46  Norfolk County Council (1999) Landscape Conservation Targeting Statement. Norwich, NCC.

47  Rural Payments Agency, Department for Environment, Food and Rural Affairs (2006) *Single Payment Scheme*. London, DEFRA publications.

48  Department of the Environment (1990) Planning Policy Guidance: Archaeology and Planning. London, HMSO, 2:26.

49  Loyd Grossman, speech at Society of Antiquaries, Burlington House, London, 17 September 2013, 'Heritage, Past, Present and Future'.

50  Chris Miele's contribution to discussion at the above conference, 17 September 2013.

# Bibliography

Allen, D.E. (1976) *The naturalist in Britain: a social history*. London, Allen Lane.

Allison, A. and Morley, J. (1989) Blakeney Point and Scolt Head Island. Norfolk, National Trust.

Armstrong, B. (1963) *Norfolk diary*. London, Hodder and Stoughton.

Ashwin, T., Bates, S. and Penn, K. (2000) *Norwich southern bypass, excavations 1989-1991*. East Anglian Archaeology 91, Gressenhall, Norfolk Museum Service.

Atkin, M. et al. (1982) *Excavations in Norwich 1971-1978*, Part 1. East Anglian Archaeology 15, Norwich, Norwich Survey in conjunction with the Scole Archaeological Committee.

Ayers, B. (1985) *Excavations within the north-east bailey of Norwich Castle*, 1979. East Anglian Archaeology 28, Norwich, Norfolk Museum Service.

Ayers, B. and Lawson, A. (1983) *Digging under the doorstep*. Norwich, Norfolk Museum Service.

Ayers, B., Bown, J. and Reeve, J. (1992) *Digging ditches*. Norwich, Norfolk Museum Service.

Ayton, J. (2012) 'The mid-twentieth century norfolk county survey and plan', *The Annual* 21, 15-32.

Ayton, J. (2013) 'The first county development plan; part 2, after the plan 1951-71', *The Annual* 22, 5-19.

Barbour, R. (2013) *Sir Thomas Browne: a life*. Oxford, Oxford University Press.

Batsford, H. (1940) *How to see the country*. London, Batsford.

Becket, G. and Bull, A. (1999) *A flora of Norfolk*. Kings Lynn, G. Becket.

Betjeman, J. (2001) 'A greatness in profusion', in C. Roberts (ed.), *Treasure for the future: a celebration of the Norfolk Churches Trust 1976-2001*. Norwich, Norfolk Churches Trust.

Blomefield, F. (1803) *An essay towards a topographical history of Norfolk*. London, William Miller.

Bournemouth University and English Heritage (1995) *The Monuments at Risk Survey of England*. London, English Heritage.

Bowden, M. (1991) *Pitt Rivers: the life and archaeological work of Lieutenant-General Pitt Rivers, DCL, FRS, FSA*. Cambridge, Cambridge University Press.

Broads Authority (2004) *Broads Plan*. Norwich, Broads Authority.

Bull, A. (1999) 'The Norfolk botanists', in G. Beckett and A. Bull, *A Flora of Norfolk*. Kings Lynn, G. Becket.

Butler, J.R.M. (1960) *Lord Lothian*. Oxford, Oxford University Press.

Bygott, J. (1923) *Eastern England*. London, Routledge.

Carson, R. (1963) *Silent Spring*. London, Hamish Hamilton.

Chinery, C. (1999) 'Population', in T. Heaton (ed.), *Norfolk century*. Norwich, Eastern Daily Press.

Clarke, D. (2008) *The country houses of Norfolk, part two: the lost houses*. Wymondham, George Reeve.

Clarke, H. and Carter, A. (1977) *Excavations in Kings Lynn 1963-1970*, Society for Medieval Archaeology Monograph 7. London, Society of Medieval Archaeology.

Clarke, W.G. (1925) *In Breckland wilds*. Cambridge, Heffers.

Countryside Commission (1972) *New agricultural landscapes*. London, HMSO.

Countryside Review Committee (1976) *The countryside: problems and policies*. London, HMSO.

Cowell, B. (2008) *The heritage obsession: the battle for England's past*. Cirencester, Tempus.

Cozens-Hardy, B. (1926) 'Scheduling of the Norfolk ancient monuments', *Norfolk Archaeology* 22, 221-7.

Cozens-Hardy, B. (1946) 'The early days of the Society', *Norfolk Archaeology* 29, 1-7.

CPRE (1975) *Landscape: the need for a public voice*. London, CPRE.

Dain, A. (2004) 'An enlightened and polite society', in C. Rawcliffe and R.G. Wilson (eds), *Norwich since 1550*. London and New York, Hambledon and London.

Davies, G.C. (1884) *Norfolk broads and rivers*, 2nd edn. Edinburgh and London, W. Blackwood and Son.

Department of the Environment (1990) Planning Policy Guidance: Archaeology and Planning. London, HMSO.

Doughty, H.M. (1897) *Summer in Broadland*. London, Jarrolds.

Dower, M. (1965) *The fourth wave: the challenge of leisure*. London, Civic Trust.

Duffy, E. (1961) 'Nature Conservation' in *BAAS Norwich and its Region*. Norwich, BAAS local executive committee.

Dutt, W.A. (1905) *The Norfolk Broads*. London, Methuen.

Dymond, D. (1985) *The Norfolk landscape*. London, Hodder and Stoughton.

Earl, J. (1996 ) 'London Government', in M. Hunter (ed.), *Preserving the past: the rise of heritage in modern Britain*. Gloucester, Alan Sutton.

Edwards, D.A. and Wade-Martins, P. (1987) *Norfolk from the Air*. Norwich, Norfolk Museums Service.

Ellis, E.A. (1965) *The Broads*. London, Collins.

Ewans, M. (1992) *The battle for the Broads*. Lavenham, Terence Dalton.

Fairbrother, N. *New lives, new landscapes*. Harmondsworth, Penguin.

Fowler, E. (1976) 'Some Norfolk naturalists', in Norfolk Naturalists Trust (ed.), *Nature in Norfolk: a heritage in trust*. Norwich, Jarrold and Sons.

Friday, L. (ed.) (1997) *Wicken Fen, the making of a wetland nature reserve*. London, Harley Books.

Fry, S. (2013) 'Saving Britain's ancient sites', *British Archaeology* March/April, 30-35.

Gay, C.E. (1944) 'Presidential address', *TNNNS* 16, 4.

Geldart, H.D. (1913) 'Presidential address', *TNNNS* 9, 643-90.

George, M. (1992) *Landuse, ecology and conservation in Broadland*. Chichester, Packard.

Goodman, N. (ed.) (2007) *Dawson Turner: a Norfolk antiquary and his remarkable family*. Chichester, Phillimore.

Greenwood, R. and Norris, M. (1976) *The brasses of Norfolk churches*. Norwich, Norfolk Churches Trust.

Grenville, J. (ed.) (1999) *Managing the historic rural landscape*. London, Routledge.

Gurney, E. and R. (1908) *The Sutton Freshwater Laboratory*. (No further details: copy in Local Studies Library, Norwich Public Library)

Harrod, W. (ed.) (n.d.) *Norfolk country churches and the future*. Norwich, Norfolk Society.

Harrod, W. and Linnell, C.L.S. (1957) *Shell guide to Norfolk*. London, Faber.

Heaton, T. (ed.) (1999) *Norfolk century*. Norwich, Eastern Daily Press.

Hoskins, W.G. (1955) *The making of the English landscape*. London, Hodder and Stoughton.

Hunter, M. (ed.) (1996) *Preserving the past: the rise of heritage in modern Britain*. Gloucester, Alan Sutton.

Impey, E. (2008) *Castle Acre Priory and Castle*. Swindon, English Heritage.

Jeans, D.N. (1990) 'Planning and the myth of the English countryside', *Rural History* 1, 261.

Jessopp, A. (1884) *The Trials of a Country Parson*. London, Fisher-Unwin.

Johnson, F. (1929) 'John Kirkpatrick, antiquary', *Norfolk Archaeology* 23, 285-304.

Kains-Jackson, C.P. (1880) *Our ancient monuments and the land around them*. London, Elliot Stock.

Ketton-Cremer, R.W. (1944) *Norfolk portraits*. London, Faber.

Ketton-Cremer, R.W. (1948) *A Norfolk gallery*. London, Faber.

Ketton Cremer, R.W. (1952) 'The rector of Fersfield', *Norfolk Archaeology* 30, 365-9.

Kirby, M. (1999) 'Nature', in T. Heaton (ed.), *Norfolk century*. Norwich, Eastern Daily Press.

Lambert, J., Jennings, J., Smith, C., Green, C. and Hutchison, J. (1960) *The making of the Broads*. Royal Geographical Society, Series 3. London, RGS.

Lawson, A.J. (1981) 'The Barrows of Norfolk', in A.J. Lawson, E.A. Martin and D. Priddy, *The Barrows of East Anglia*. East Anglian Archaeology 12, Gressenhall, Norfolk Museums Service.

Lowe, P. (1989) 'The rural idyll defended: from preservation to conservation', in G.E. Mingay (ed.), *The rural idyll*. London, Routledge.

Lowe, P., Cox, C., MacEwen, M., O'Rioden, T. and Winter, M. (1986) *Countryside conflicts: the politics of farming, forestry and conservation*. Aldershot, Gower.

Matless, D., Watkins, C. and Merchant, P. (2010) 'Nature trails: the production of an instructive landscape in Britain', *Rural History* 21:1, 97-131.

McKitterick, D. (2007) 'Dawson Turner and his book collecting', in N. Goodman (ed.), *Dawson Turner: a Norfolk antiquary and his remarkable family*. Chichester, Phillimore.

Moore, N.W. (1987) *The bird of time: the science and politics of nature conservation - a personal account*. Cambridge, Cambridge University Press.

Mynors, C. (2006) *Listed buildings, conservation areas and monuments*, 4th edn. London, Thomson, Sweet and Maxwell.

National Farmers' Union and Country Landowners' Association (1987) *Caring for the countryside*. London, NFU and CLA.

Newby, H. (1988) *The countryside in question*. London, Hutchison.

Ninham, H. (1864) *Views of the ancient city gates of Norwich as they appeared in 1722*. Norwich, Cundill, Miller and Leavins.

Norfolk County Council (1951) *Development plan for the county of Norfolk*. Norwich, NCC.

Norfolk County Council (1978) *Norfolk structure plan*. Norwich, NCC.

Norfolk County Council (1994) *Norfolk countryside conservation strategy*. Norwich, NCC.

Norfolk County Council (1999) Landscape Conservation Targeting Statement. Norwich, NCC.

Norfolk County Council, Broads Consortium (1971) *Broadland study and plan*. Norwich, NCC

Norfolk Naturalists Trust (ed.) (1976) *Nature in Norfolk: a heritage in trust*. Norwich, Jarrold and Sons.

Oliver, F.W. (1926-27) 'Nature reserves', *TNNNS* 12:3, 317-18.

Owen, D.M. (1984) *The making of Kings Lynn: a documentary survey*. Oxford, Oxford University Press for the British Academy.

Owen, J. (2013) *Darwin's apprentice: an archaeological biography of John Lubbock*. Barnsley, Pen and Sword Archaeology.

Oxford Archaeological Unit (1999) *Management of archaeological sites in arable landscapes*. Oxford, OAU.

Paget, P. (1972) 'How the Scheme for Redundant Churches is meant to work', in W. Harrod (ed.), *Norfolk Country Churches and the Future*. Holt, The Norfolk Society.

Parker, V. (1971) *The making of Kings Lynn: secular buildings from the 11th to the 17th century*. Chichester, Phillimore.

Parliamentary Papers (1947a) Report of the National Parks Committee (England and Wales) (The Hobhouse Report). Command Paper 7121, London, HMSO.

Parliamentary Papers (1947b) Report on the Conservation of Nature in England and Wales (the Huxley Report). Command Paper 7122, London, HMSO.

Parliamentary Papers (1966-68) Report of the Committee of Enquiry into the arrangements for the protection of field monuments (The Walshe Report). Command Paper 3904, London, HMSO.

Paterson, H. and Wade-Martins, P. (1999) 'Monument conservation in Norfolk', in J. Grenville (ed.), *Managing the historic rural landscape*. London, Routledge.

Patterson, A. (1905) *Wildfowlers and poachers*. London, Methuen.

Pevsner, N. and Wilson, B. (1997) *Buildings of England: Norfolk*, 2 vols. London, Penguin.

Piggott, S. (1976) *Ruins in a landscape*. Edinburgh, Edinburgh University Press.

Pilfold, W. (2007) 'Defending farmland', in B. Short, C. Watkins and J. Martin, *The front line of freedom*. Exeter, British Agricultural History Society.

Popescu, S. (2009) *Norwich Castle: excavations and historical survey, 1987-1998*. East Anglian Archaeology 9, Gressenhall, Norfolk Museums Service.

Rackham, O. (1986) *The history of the countryside*. London, J.M. Dent.

Rainbird Clarke, R. (1960) *East Anglia*. London, Thames and Hudson.

Rawcliffe, C. and Wilson, R. (eds) (2004) *Norwich since 1550*. London and New York, Hambledon and London.

Rigold, S.E. (1962-3) 'The Anglian cathedral of North Elmham, Norfolk', *Medieval Archaeology* 6-7, 53-66.

Roberts, C. (ed.), *Treasure for the future: a celebration of the Norfolk Churches Trust 1976-2001*. Norwich, Norfolk Churches Trust.

Rodziewicz, J. (2013) 'Making a museum out of a Norman keep and Victorian prison: The Norfolk and Norwich Museum 1886-1896', *Norfolk Archaeology* 46, 503-10.

Rotherham, I. (2013) *The lost fens: England's greatest ecological disaster*. London, The History Press.

Rothschild, M. (1983) *Dear Lord Rothschild*. London, Hutchison.

Roulett, J. (1983) 'Late Victorian environmental organisations', *Victorian Studies* 26, 197-222.

Rowell, T.A. (1997) 'The history of the fen', in L. Friday (ed.) *Wicken Fen, the making of a wetland nature reserve*. London, Harley Books.

Rural Payments Agency, Department for Environment, Food and Rural Affairs (2006) *Single Payment Scheme*. London, DEFRA publications.

Saunders, A.D. (1983) 'A century of ancient monument legislation, 1882-1983', *Antiquaries Journal* 63, 18.

Scott, Lord Justice (1942) Report of the Committee of Land Utilisation in Rural Areas. Command Paper 6278, London, HMSO.

Serpell, M.F. (1983) 'Sir John Fenn, his friends and the Paston Letters', *Antiquaries Journal* 63:1, 95-121.

Sheail, J. (1976) *Nature in trust*. Glasgow and London, Blaikie.

Sheail, J. (1998) *Nature conservation in Britain*. London, HMSO.

Sheail, J. (2002) *Environmental history of the twentieth century*. Basingstoke, Palgrave.

Shoard, M. (1971) *The theft of the countryside*. Aldershot, Temple Smith.

St J. O'Neil, B.H. (1946) 'The Congress of Archaeological Societies', *Antiquaries Journal* 26, 61-6.

Stephen, G.A. (1921) 'Francis Blomefield's queries in preparation for his History of Norfolk', *Norfolk Archaeology* 20, 1-10.

Stevenson, H. (1872) 'Presidential address', *TNNNT* 1:3, 7-19.

Street, A.G. (1937) 'The countryman's view', in C. Williams-Ellis (ed.), *Britain and the beast*. London, J.M. Dent.

Tansley, A.G. (ed.) (1911) *Types of British vegetation*. London, Central Committee for the Survey and Study of British Vegetation.

Tansley, A.G. (1945) *Our heritage and wild nature: a plea for organised nature conservation*. Cambridge, Cambridge University Press.

Thurley, S. (2013) *Men from the ministry: how Britain saved its heritage*. Newhaven and London, Yale University Press.

*Victoria County History, Norfolk* (1901) Volume 1. London, Constable.

Vincent, J.E (1907) *Through East Anglia in a motor car*. London, Methuen.

Wade Martins, S. and Williamson, T. (2008) *The countryside of East Anglia: changing landscapes 1870-1950*. Woodbridge, Boydell and Brewer.

Wade-Martins, P. (1996) 'Monument Preservation through Land Purchase', *Conservation Bulletin* 29, 7-13.

Wade-Martins, P. (1999) 'Discovering our past', in T. Heaton (ed.), *Norfolk century*. Norwich, Eastern Daily Press.

Wade-Martins, P. (2008) 'Managing Archaeological Sites in Norfolk', *Conservation Land Management* 6, 14-18.

Wade-Martins, P. (2014) 'An experiment in conservation: the early years of the Norfolk Archaeological Trust' in Ashley, S. and Marsden, A., *Landscape and Artifacts*, 235-249, Archaeopress, Oxford.

Walpole, J. (1997) *Art and artists of the Norwich School*. Woodbridge, Antique Collectors' Club.

Ward Lock and Co. (n.d) *The Broads*. London.

Waterson, M. (1994) *The National Trust: the first hundred years*. London, BBC/National Trust.

Waterson, M. (2011) *A noble thing: the National Trust and its benefactors*. London, Scala Publishers.

White, W. (1883) *History, Gazetteer, and Directory of Norfolk*. London: Simpkin, Marshall, & Co.

Williams, R. (1973) *The country and the city*. London, Chatto and Windus.

Williams-Ellis, C. (ed.) (1937) *Britain and the beast*. London, J.M. Dent.

Williamson, T. (1997) *The Norfolk Broads: a landscape history*. Manchester, Manchester University Press.

Woodson-Boulton, A. (2008) 'Victorian museums and Victorian society', *History Compass* 6, 109-46.

Wright, P. (2009) *On living in an old country*. Oxford, Oxford University Press.

Yanni, C. (2005) *Nature's museums: Victorian science and the architecture of display*. New York, Princeton University Press.

Young, E.W. (1996) *Sixty years of the Norfolk Society*. Norwich, Norfolk Society.

# Index